STARVING AMIDST TOO MUCH

& Other IWW Writings on the FOOD INDUSTRY

by

T-Bone Slim, L. S. Chumley,
Jim Seymour & Jack Sheridan

Edited & Introduced by
Peter Rachleff

Foreword by Carlos Cortez

CHICAGO
Charles H. Kerr Publishing Company
2005

The cover illustration,
by IWW cartoonist "Dust" Wallin,
originally appeared in the
pamphlet by L. S. Chumley
reprinted in this volume.

FIRST EDITION

ISBN 088286-303-7
(paper)

Thanks to
Ruth Sheridan and Harry Sheridan
for information, documents, and encouragement,
and to Jen Besemer, Julie Herrada,
Ruth Oppenheim-Rothschild,
and Tamara Smith
for technical assistance.

WANTED

For future publishing projects: Photos, publications, artwork, memorabilia, and ephemera concerning the IWW, anarchism, the early Socialist Party; Bughouse Square, Hobo College, the Dil Pickle Club, and other free-speech forums; and early Charles H. Kerr publications. Please write to the address below, or leave a message at 773-465-7774.

Write for our free catalog.
CHARLES H. KERR PUBLISHING COMPANY
Established 1886
1740 West Greenleaf Avenue
Chicago IL 60626

Fast food work

is now indistinguishable
from the assembly line work
of most manufacturing industries.
The biggest differences are the youth
of fast food workers and the low level of their wages.
Automation and efficiency combine
with the low wages and benefits
to make the fast food industry very profitable.

But there is more going on in this industry
than exploitation and regimentation.
Despite, or because of, the harsh conditions,
young workers are learning about alienated labor,
class conflict, and collectivity.

The pamphlets, columns, and articles collected
in this volume are far more than historical artifacts.
They offer today's readers analyses, strategies,
tactics, humor, and inspiration.
T-Bone Slim, L. S. Chumley, Jim Seymour
and Jack Sheridan
not only spoke to the workers of their eras,
but they speak to the workers of the present and the future.

From the Introduction by

PETER RACHLEFF

Peter Rachleff discovered and joined the IWW as a college student in the early 1970s and has been an on-again/off-again red card carrier over the years. Since 1982 he has taught labor history at Macalester College in St Paul, Minnesota, and has continued to be an activist within the labor movement, locally and nationally. In the mid-1980s, he served as chairperson of the Twin Cities Support Committee for UFCW Local P-9, which was striking against the Hormel meat-packing company, and he later wrote a book about that strike (*Hard-Pressed in the Heartland: The Hormel Strike and the Future of the Labor Movement*). His articles have appeared in *Radical America*, *Socialist Revolution*, *Labor Notes*, *Labor History*, *Labour/Le Travail*, *Z Magazine*, *New Labor Forum*, and the *International Socialist Review*.

STARVING AMIDST TOO MUCH

By T-BONE SLIM

Poets and Pearls
- A Rhapsody -

Recipes for Health
- Scientific -

PRICE FIFTEEN CENTS

The original cover of T-Bone Slim's 1923 pamphlet;
Starving Amidst Too Much
(cartoonist unknown)

TABLE OF CONTENTS

An IWW "Silent Agitator" Sticker

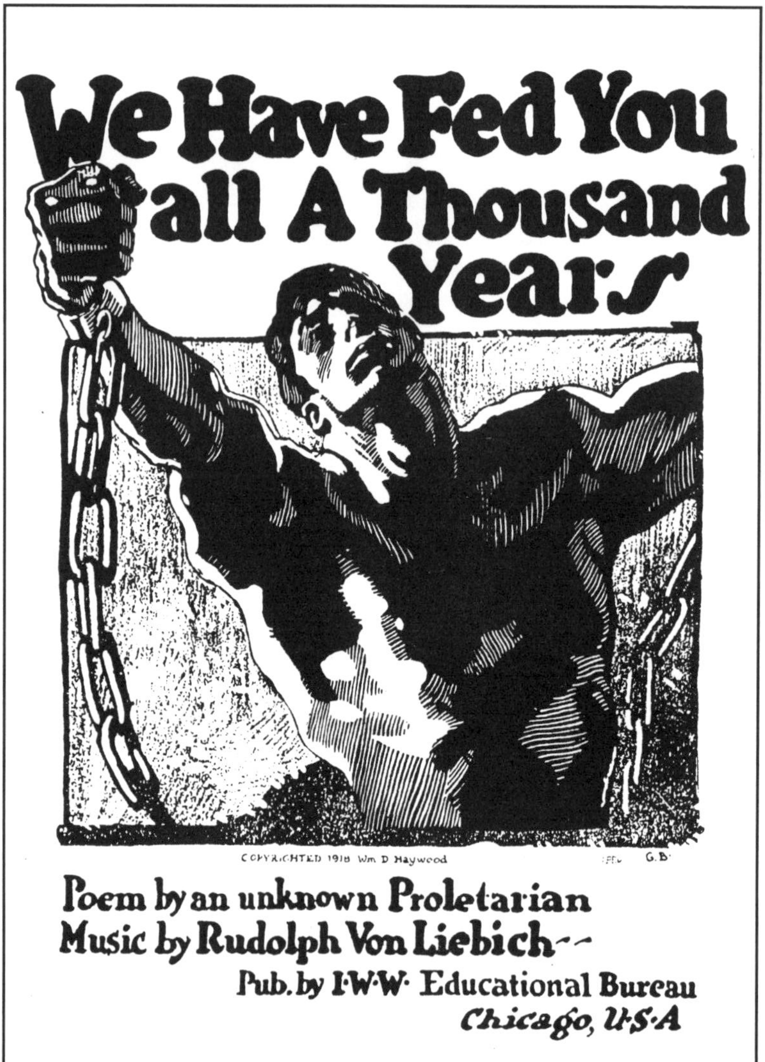

Sheet Music for a Popular IWW Song

CARLOS CORTEZ

Foreword:

IWW Writings on Food & the Food Industry

My good friend Jack Sheridan was a longstanding fixture in the Chicago branch of the Industrial Workers of the World. He and his twin brother Jimmie had attended their first IWW meeting as children in the 1910s, brought by their father who was himself an IWW supporter as well as a militant in the local Painters' Union. All three were gifted soapboxers at Chicago's famous outdoor free-speech forum in Washington Square (better known as Bughouse Square), across the street from The Newberry Library. Often called "The Terrible Sheridans," the trio were also mainstays at the nearby IWW-influenced Dil Pickle Club, "the indoor Bughouse Square." Well into the 1950s, long after the old man had passed away, Jack and Jimmie continued to hold forth at the Square, promoting the revolutionary program of the IWW.

Jack, the more bombastic of the twins, was a unique personality and a man of many accomplishments. A "road scholar" in the great Wobbly tradition, he hoboed all across North America. He was also a true Chicago "forum bug"—a popular presence at such outposts of free-speech as The Seven Arts, the Social Science Institute, the Pindarians, the Druids Society (a literary/political discussion club that he cofounded), the open forum at Third Unitarian Church, Slim Brundage's College of Complexes (the old Dil Pickle's most noted successor), and of course the IWW's own forums. A seasoned debater and spirited conversationalist, in the 1950s he hosted a TV show on handwriting analysis. (He may well have been the first card-carrying Wob on what was then a new medium.)

A poet himself, and a powerful reciter of poetry, for several years Jack also edited the New York-based poetry magazine, *The Raven Anthology*. Manuscripts of some of his unpublished poems and essays, as well as a novel, are deposited in the Labadie Collection of the University of Michigan Library in Ann Arbor.

His wide-ranging interests and activities notwithstanding, Jack's main cause throughout his life was the IWW, and he remained true to the union's aims and principles to the end. As a writer he frequently brightened the pages of such varied publications as *The Hobo News*, *Amazing Stories*, and the *Chicago Daily News*, but his contributions to the IWW press outweigh all the rest. In addition to his many articles in the *Industrial Worker*, he also wrote for the *One Big Union Monthly* in the 1930s and for the Chicago IWW branch journal, *The Rebel Worker* in the 1960s. He was a "regular" at Chicago branch meetings, and a featured speaker at Joe Hill Memorials and other union events. When a sizeable number of young workers rallied to the IWW in the mid-1960s, it was Jack who gave them their first lessons in soapboxing at Bughouse Square.

My late companion Marianna and I both wept at Fellow Worker Sheridan's funeral, where it was my task to give his final send-off.

* * *

In fall 1959 Jack wrote the excellent series of articles titled "Breakfast With Destiny" for the *Industrial Worker*. With a soapboxer's zest for the well-told tale, his IWW critical spirit, and always vivid humor, he unraveled the complex stories underlying our everyday lives—even something as seemingly simple as the food and drink on our morning table. Impressed by his interpretation of how human history was really shaped, I tried to convince my friends on the board of the Charles H. Kerr Publishing Company to reissue the series as a pamphlet.

Then the idea expanded: Why not do an entire *book* of IWW writings on food and the food industry? A volume with selections by T-Bone Slim, Leland S. Chumley and Jim Seymour appeared all the more appropriate in that Jack in all probability was personally acquainted with all of these Fellow Workers.

In a very real sense, then, Jack Sheridan inspired this book.

To scholar/activist Peter Rachleff we are indebted not only for putting this diverse material into a useful historical perspective, but also for his contributions toward updating the IWW critique in this period of fast-food, junk-food, union-busting, genetic engineering, globalization and ecological devastation. Along the way he drives home a crucial point: however much the food industry has changed since the articles in this book were written, the tried-and-true Wobbly methods of self-organization, direct action, on-the-job democracy and solidarity are still what the workers need to win.

Needless to say, I feel honored to have been asked to write this Foreword. As Peter Rachleff emphasizes, what the Wobblies of yesteryear had to say about the all-important "food question" is still relevant in our time. These writings clearly deserve wider circulation, and should be considered and discussed by working people today.

To make such writings available is in line not only with the aims of the IWW, but also of the Charles H. Kerr Publishing Company.

Chicago, 2004

IWW "Silent Agitator" Sticker

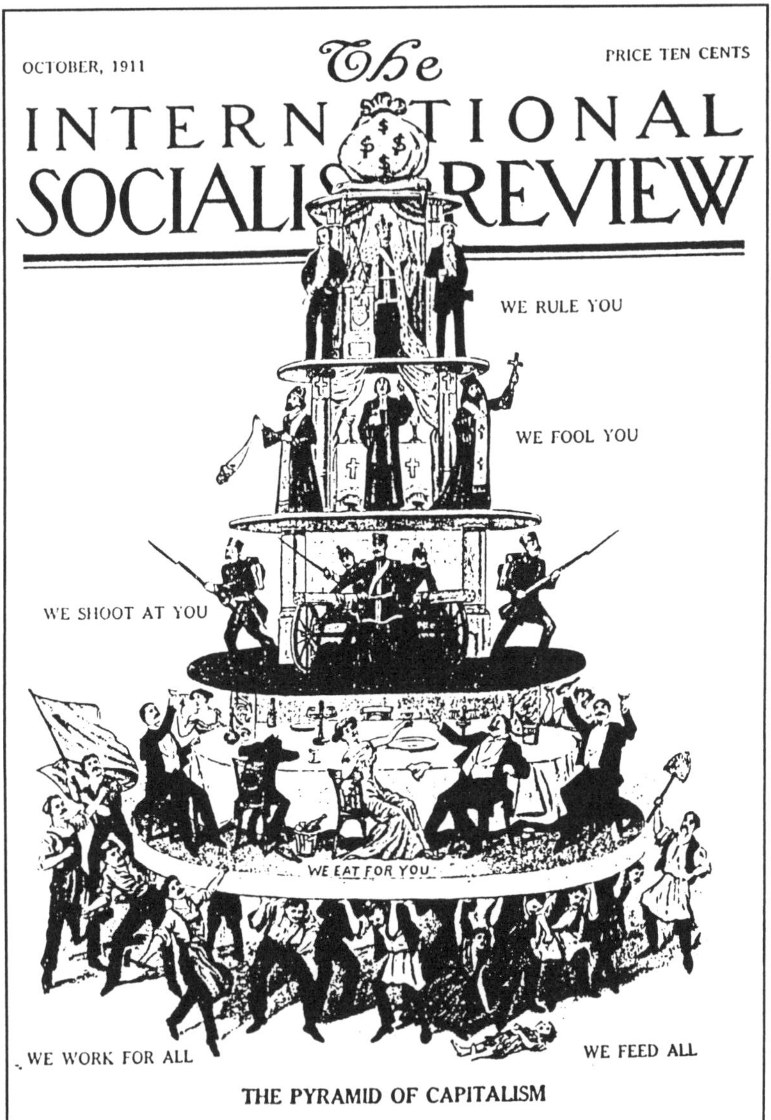

THE PYRAMID OF CAPITALISM
(*International Socialist Review*, October 1911)

PETER RACHLEFF

Introduction:
Making and Breaking the Food Chain(s)

Welcome to the Food Industry

What was your first job? Did you have a sense of achievement that you could do the job, function in a strange environment, and provide or produce something useful? Did you also learn about selling your time, freedom and unfreedom, producing profits for your boss, supporting your co-workers and getting their support? Remember that first paycheck, how good it felt to have money in your pocket to spend the way you wanted to spend it, and, then, that nagging voice that said: "Is this all I'm worth?" A lot of mixed feelings, mixed lessons, swirled together in that first job.

Nowadays, fast food jobs are the most common first jobs for teenagers. About two-thirds of this nation's fast food workers are under the age of twenty. That first experience—of collective work and alienated labor, exploitation and resistance, monotony and empowerment—comes for many of us at McDonald's, Wendy's, Burger King, Taco Bell, and other fast food chains.

Work in the fast food industry is highly routinized, fragmented, and regimented. "The ethos of the assembly line remains at its core," writes Eric Schlosser in his best-selling *Fast Food Nation*." Powdered, dehydrated, and frozen ingredients are brought back to life with the adding of water or fiery heat, syrups are magically transformed into shakes and sodas, and uniformly sized and shaped potato strips are deep-fried in meat fats to become "french fries," facilitated by conveyor belts and automated machines, the products at many stages untouched by human hands. "The fast food industry's obsession with throughput [turning raw materials into finished products as efficiently as possible] has altered the way millions of Americans work, turned commercial kitchens into small factories, and changed familiar foods into commodities that are manufactured." [1]

There was an ironic truth at the core of the Bush administration's proposal in early 2004 to reclassify fast food work from "service" to "manufacturing." Critics were quick to point out that Bush was trying to cover up the 2.7 million manufacturing jobs lost since the start of his presidency, a loss due to recession, off-shoring and out-sourcing, automation, and deindustrialization. Of course, Bush's critics were right. But there can be no denying that fast food work is now indistinguishable from the assembly line work of most manufacturing industries. The biggest differences are the youth of fast food workers and the low level of their wages. Indeed, the fast food industry pays a higher percentage of its workers minimum wage than any other industry.[2]

Automation and efficiency combine with the low wages and benefits to make the fast food industry very profitable. With these profits, fast food's corporate owners have purchased professional sports franchises, endowed chairs at universities (mostly in Business departments), and emerged as some of our country's most visible "philanthropists." Meanwhile, low wage workers cycle in and out of their workplaces at turnover rates of 300 to 400%. The average fast food worker lasts four months on her or his first job.[3]

But there is more going on in this industry than exploitation and regimentation. Despite, or because of, the harsh conditions, young workers are learning about alienated labor, class conflict, and collectivity. Listen to historian and activist Robin D.G. Kelley as he describes his first work experience at McDonald's in his book, *Race Rebels*:

> "McDonald's is a happy place." I really believed that slogan when I began working there in 1978. For many of us employed at the central Pasadena franchise, Mickey D's meant food, folks, and fun, though our main objective was *funds*. Don't get me wrong; the work was tiring and the polyester uniforms unbearable. The swing managers, who made slightly more than the rank-and-file, were constantly on our ass to move fast and smile more frequently. The customers treated us as if we were stupid, probably because 90 percent of the employees were African Americans or Chicanos from poor families. But we found inventive ways to compensate. Like virtually all of my fellow workers, I liberated McDonaldland cookies by the boxful, volunteered to clean "lots and lobbies" in order to talk to my friends, and accidentally cooked too many Quarter Pounders and apple

pies near closing time, knowing fully well that we could take home whatever was left over. Sometimes we (mis)used the available technology to our advantage. Back in our day, the shakes did not come ready mixed. We had to pour the frozen shake mix from the shake machine into a paper cup, add flavored syrup, and place it on an electric blender for a couple of minutes. If it was not attached correctly, the mixer blade would cut the sides of the cup and cause a disaster. While these mishaps slowed us down and created a mess to clean up, anyone with an extra cup handy got a little shake out of it.

> Because we were underpaid and overworked, we accepted consumption as just compensation—though in hindsight eating Big Macs and fries to make up for low wages and mistreatment was probably closer to self-flagellation.[4]

Kelley calls this kind of resistance "infrapolitics," a "hidden transcript" of "many battles to roll back constraints and exercise some power over, or create some space within, the institutions and social relations that dominate our lives."[5] Such politics are often expressed informally and individually, and they may even be hidden behind "masks" of apparent contentment. These dynamics can have diverse cumulative effects—from the demoralization of those who wear the mask for too long to shifting the balance of power (what historian Carter Goodrich long ago called an invisible "frontier of control," where management's authority stopped and workers' autonomy began) in workers' favor. The same dynamics can occasionally provide the energy, vision, and direction among workers to create permanent organizations, such as unions.[6]

Workers Organizing and Organizing Workers

Indeed, food industry workers of all sorts—from farm workers, cannery workers, and packinghouse workers, at one end of the food chain, to waiters, waitresses, cooks, bartenders, and hotel workers at the other end—have a long history of self-organization, dating from the commodification of food (making it something we buy rather than grow or catch for ourselves) and the commercialization of meals (eating out for a price rather than cooking for ourselves, our families, and friends). Work in the industries which provided foodstuffs or meals logically followed the capitalist rules of organization which were being applied in diverse industries: a division of labor; the introduction of machinery to deskill, regiment, and control labor; the centralization of authority; the measurement of time and its expression in money; for those providing services, an expectation—reinforced by tips—that they provide emotional labor; an unwillingness by employers to invest in safe, healthy, and pleasant working conditions; and, unless workers' organizations emerge, intervene, and impose improvements, a tendency over time to see all these conditions and circumstances worsen. Moreover, these conditions within workplaces have often produced foodstuffs and meals which endanger the health of consumers, even as lower prices and access to greater variety is touted.[7]

In the late 19th century, some food industry workers were seen as—and saw themselves as—"skilled," from a minority of packinghouse workers and butchers in retail shops to cooks and chefs in high-end restaurants in larger cities. These skilled food industry workers began to organize themselves in craft unions, often affiliated with the American Federation of Labor. These new unions rarely reached out to other food industry workers (the "unskilled," immigrants, workers of color, women) and they were little able to protect their members from the continuing transformation and reorganization of both their industries and their work processes. On some occasions, they were able to garner the support of consumers or those other skilled workers who were also organized and connected to the AFL, but, on the whole, their economic security and status slid steadily downhill.[8]

In the 1910s and 20s, the Industrial Workers of the World (IWW or "Wobblies") inspired waiters, waitresses, and cooks to try a different model of labor organization and different tactics. Founded in 1905, the IWW promoted industrial rather than craft organization. They sought to organize precisely those workers—the poor, the migratory, the marginalized—who were deemed by the skilled workers of the AFL to be "unorganizable." The Wobblies insisted that workers' strengths lay in unity and solidarity, in the bringing together of all workers employed in the same place, even in the same industry, regardless of skill, ethnicity, race, or gender. They practiced their philosophy of "One Big Union" wherever they organized. They also urged workers to practice "direct action"—collective action in the workplace itself, used immediately to confront immediate grievances. The tactics of "direct action" could range from slowdowns, work stoppages, and "sabotage" (what one prominent Wobbly activist, Elizabeth Gurley Flynn, called "the conscious withdrawal of efficiency") to waitresses informing customers of the adulteration of foods and the unhealthfulness of kitchen conditions. The IWW also employed cultural activism—parades, songs, pageants, cartoons, and soapbox speaking—to build unity among its members and to seek the support of the wider community.[9]

The IWW had a dramatic history. They inspired hundreds of thousands, if not millions, of workers, giving them a new vision of not only themselves but also of their ability to imagine and build a new society. Workers of all sorts took to heart such slogans as "An Injury to One is an Injury to All" and "Give us Bread, but Give us Roses, Too." They practiced solidarity, stood up to their bosses and the government, and fought for increased power on the job and an improved standard of living in their communities. Not surprisingly, the Wobblies attracted the hostility of employers and the government, and they were the subject of negative media campaigns, blacklisting, and ferocious police and military repression. Although the union grew numerically despite the persecution—reaching its peak membership in 1923-24—mounting harassment hampered its on-the-job effectiveness. With the passage of "criminal syndicalism" laws (in effect, laws against union organizing, applied almost exclusively against the IWW) and the jailing of hundreds of its best organizers, few locals achieved much stability, and the organization as a whole declined after 1925.[10]

Nevertheless, the IWW had some stunning breakthroughs and the workers they influenced continued to practice its key ideas and tactics over the course of their lives in the workforce and the labor movement. Throughout the 1920s and 1930s, IWW activists and ex-IWW activists led and contributed to efforts to build militant local and national unions.[11]

The IWW began organizing in the food industry in the years before World War I. They insisted that workers in this industry were "essential and ... destined to play an important role in the struggles between those who work and those who own."[12] They urged skilled workers to abandon craft unionism and embrace their lesser-skilled fellow workers, even if they were of different races, ethnicities, or genders. They called attention to the miserable working conditions, low pay and abuse faced by the workers, the indignities caused by the tipping system, and the particular exploitation that young workers and women workers experienced. The Wobblies put forward solidarity as the best answer to the challenges faced by food industry workers and they offered a variety of configurations—the Hotel, Restaurant, and Domestic Workers' Industrial Union, the Hotel Workers' Industrial Union, and the Food Stuff Workers' Industrial Union, among others—for food industry workers to join. They made some headway in Chicago and launched a dramatic strike in New York City in the summer of 1912, but built little permanent organization.[13]

Over the next decades, food industry workers continued their efforts to organize, often building on the Wobblies' vision of industrial unionism and their direct action tactics, to which they added efforts to connect with the consumers of their services. In New York City, the Hotel Employees and Restaurant Employees Union (HERE) in the 1920s turned to the Women's Trade Union League and its largely middle class members for help in passing legislation limiting overtime hours and raising minimum wages, while in the 1930s they participated in Minimum Wage Clubs, which united low wage workers across a variety of industries to fight for laws to raise wages. By the 1940s and 1950s, they had reached a high level of unionization in major cities, converting high turnover jobs into stable employment for many women. When the United Cannery, Agricultural, and Packinghouse Workers of America (UCAPAWA) and the Food, Tobacco, Agricultural, and Allied Workers' Union (FTA-CIO) organized white and Mexican and Mexican-American workers in the Southwest or white and African American workers in the South in the 1930s and 1940s, they made racial justice, civil rights, and community organizing central to their efforts. In the late 1940s, the United Packinghouse Workers of America not only fought for racial justice, but they also argued for the perpetuation of WWII price controls on food products.[14]

In the 1960s, inspired by the civil rights and anti-Vietnam War movements as well as the emerging youth-oriented counterculture, the IWW experienced a notable resurgence, particularly in Chicago and the San Francisco Bay Area. In both places, the organization of food industry workers was a central expression of this revival. The prospect of organizing dishwashers and other restaurant workers was discussed in the debut issue (May Day 1964) of the Chicago IWW Branch magazine, *The Rebel Worker,* and its next issue chronicled the IWW's first agricultural workers' strike in decades (Michigan blueberry pickers, summer '64). During the next few years workers at "Alice's Revisited" and several other small restaurants in the pre-gentrified Lincoln Park area of the city organized in the IWW.

In San Francisco, meanwhile, the Wobblies led a coffee-house strike that lasted for weeks and captured the public imagination. In Berkeley Wobs organized the Florentine Café and several other popular student gathering-places.

Also in the '60s, the United Farm Workers of America inspired a nationwide consumer boycott of non-union grapes and lettuce, building a Wobbly-inflected movement culture. In this long battle, California Wobs were especially active, and one of them—Eugene Nelson—wrote an early and influential memoir of the struggle: the book *Huelga* (Strike).[15]

More recently, a coalition of college student activists and the United Steel Workers of America has launched an international economic pressure and boycott campaign against Coca-Cola ("Killer Coke") for its ferocious anti-unionism in Colombia, including the murder of union activists. In the summer of 2004, Starbucks workers in New York City joined the IWW and won a union election, only to have the results set aside by the National Labor Relations Board, who told them that they could not organize just one Starbucks shop![16]

Frank Ellis & the IUAW

A particularly inspiring example is provided by the experience of the Wobbly-influenced Independent Union of All Workers (IUAW), which emerged in the Austin, Minnesota, Hormel plant in 1933, spread to workers in the Austin area (including waiters, waitresses, cooks, and even retail workers), and then spread to 13 other cities across the upper Midwest. IUAW promoted a model of "wall-to-wall" unionism, before being dismantled by a variety of internal and external pressures into diverse component parts in 1937-1938. The IUAW was the brainchild of Frank Ellis, an itinerant packinghouse worker who had joined the IWW in the 1910s and been elected to its General Executive Board in the early 1920s. In the late 1920s, Ellis had hired into the Hormel plant and began connecting with other activists to build an "IWW-style" union, embodying internal democracy, strong shopfloor organization, direct action, an industrial structure, and solidarity among workers. Ellis was reported by fellow activists to have said: "If you fill any position in the food chain, for that matter, if you eat food, you all belong in the same union."[17]

In Austin, the union reached its goal of 100 percent unionization. It included "units" of truckers and warehouse workers, barbers and beauticians, waiters, waitresses, and bartenders, construction tradesmen and laborers, WPA laborers, automobile mechanics and service station attendants, laundry and dry cleaning workers, retail clerks and municipal employees. One of the IUAW's first actions was to picket the plant in support of local farmers, members of the Farm Holiday Association, who were seeking higher prices for their hogs in the fall of 1933. Two years later, IUAW members conducted a "shop in" at local department stores, clogging check out lanes and refusing to unload their carts until cash register clerks were given a union contract.

The IUAW built its strength through a variety of tactics. They produced a number of newspapers which they distributed widely. At times, they relied on the direct action of workers in key industries. During strikes, IUAW members in other industries provided material aid to strikers and their families. The expansion of the IUAW also rested on the collective consuming power of the Hormel workers, expressed through consumer boycotts. They also sought allies outside the boundaries of the formal labor movement, such as family farmers, hit hard by the depression. IUAW activists brought their methods into other communities in southern Minnesota, Iowa, South and North Dakota, and Wisconsin. Many of the rank-and-file packinghouse workers (not just from Austin's Hormel plant, but also from Wilson plants in Albert Lea and

Faribault, and smaller plants in Mason City, Fort Dodge, Cedar Rapids, and Ottumwa, Iowa) put in long hours as volunteer union organizers. While 100% "wall-to-wall" unionization might not have been reached in all of these outlying communities, the principles of solidarity, direct action, and union democracy sank roots among workers throughout the food industry chain—farmers and farm workers, poultry and packinghouse workers, food service and retail workers, and waiters, waitresses, and cooks. Ellis's vision—and the IWW's—had been, for a glorious and exemplary moment, realized.

A Living Legacy

Much has changed since the heyday of the Industrial Workers of the World in the 1910s or the breakthrough of the Independent Union of All Workers in the 1930s. Unions which embodied many of their values and tactics gained a position within American industrial society in the 1940s and 1950s, only to become incorporated into a "social contract" with employers and the government (that is, a tacit agreement to play by certain rules). Many of these unions were then transformed into "business unions," in which full-time officers, staff, lobbyists, and lawyers made up a bureaucracy to provide "services" to union members in exchange for dues-generated salaries. In this "service model," the soul of unions atrophied and new generations of union members learned little of the struggles of labor history. Then, when the industrial battlefield shifted in the late 1970s with globalization and economic neoliberalism, unions appeared to be hollowed out shells for whom the moniker "organized labor" served as a bitter metaphor. The unionized segment of the workforce dropped from one in three in the 1950s to one in seven in the first decade of the 21st century, and their ability to command respect and economic rewards withered simultaneously.[18]

But much, also, has not changed. As at the beginning of the 20th century, employers today push workers to work harder and put in longer hours, for which they receive inadequate pay and little economic security. The dominant culture renders workers invisible and offers only the crudest caricatures of them for popular consumption. The poor are blamed for their own poverty, while government programs to provide a social safety net are demonized. The government flexes its military might and political muscle to make the world safe for American investments, through which businesses can expand and increase their riches. And workers—particularly the white men in their midst—are encouraged to blame scapegoats (immigrants, racial minorities, assertive women, Arabs, Muslims, to name only a few) for their trials and tribulations.[19]

The pamphlets, columns, and articles collected in this volume make available to us the rich wellspring of ideas which nourished the IUAW's founder Frank Ellis—and can nourish our vision. These are far more than historical artifacts. They offer today's readers – especially those workers throughout the food industry – analyses, strategies, tactics, humor, and inspiration. T-Bone Slim, L.S. Chumley, Jim Seymour and Jack Sheridan not only spoke to the workers of their eras, but they speak to the workers of the present and the future.

These Wobbly activists were not only labor organizers. They were also poets, cartoonists, artists, songwriters, and public speakers. They lived multidimensional lives from which they saw workers as full human beings, not merely wage-earners, creators of surplus-value, or "the rank-and-file." In their eyes and imaginations, working women and men had brains as well as hands, dreams as well as nightmares, and passions as well as energy. They encouraged workers to think not only about their exploitation but also about their pleasures, not only their lives on the job but also their lives in their communities, and, above all, to maintain their intellectual independence. They modeled for their fellow workers not only how to do this, but how to do this with a sense of humor. As a result, whether their words were penned in 1918, the 1950s, or the 1990s, they still speak to us.

In *Starving Amidst Too Much* the popular Wobbly poet and humorist T-Bone Slim takes a job as a "pearl diver" (dishwasher) in order to offer his readers an inside report on conditions in the commercialized kitchen. He emphasizes the ways that this work mirrors industrial work, from its intense division of labor, its boss-driven pressure to speed up, its piece work pay schemes, and its unsanitary working conditions. It all "drives a man to act like a squirrel in a revolving cage," he writes, "going like hell—arriving nowhere." Unless, of course, that man finds his way to "an industrial union built by the workers."[20]

In his inimitable style, Slim mixes reality and metaphors, speaking to us from a variety of vantage points within the heart of the food processing industry—restaurant kitchens, bakeries, and meatpacking plants. "...Nature ... never intended the juices for one man and the pulp for another... To separate one from the other is to break Nature's laws." If we're too slow on the uptake, he offers us a more explicit analysis:

> All of our troubles have the same source – the profit system. It is easy to understand: When too many profits go to the few, the many will become poor; and when the "few" who enjoy the profits become too numerous, then the "many" must suffer a want for the very things which they produce.

Slim continues to mix his metaphors seamlessly and effectively. "[F]ood is the internal fuel" we all need, but some foods can make us sick, while others can make us strong. "The only way to keep well (and you're sick) is to join the Industrial Workers of the World and do away with the foods that are making you sick; that is making everybody sick; that is making the whole world 'sick—and tired.'"

Chumley warns (in 1918) that the tipping system encourages workers to take on "servile, slavish, mealy-mouthed and beggarly qualities, ...the qualities desired in servants." Is this any less true today? Chumley offers a strategy against the demeaning system of tipping, focusing attention not on the employers of these workers, but on these workers themselves. "It is through disobedience that progress has been made, through disobedience and rebellion," he writes. "Disobedience in the eyes of anyone who has read history is man's original virtue." It is through refusing servitude and building organization with one's fellow workers that regaining self-respect and securing a decent material life become possible.[21]

Chumley takes his readers on a tour of the working and living conditions of food industry workers, domestics, and hotel workers in the metropolises of New York and Chicago in the 1910s. He paints a sordid picture, but one that is not unfamiliar to today's workers: waitresses who must fight off fanny-pinching customers and leering bosses; fast food workers who fear violent robberies at closing time; hotel maids expected to clean up blood, vomit, and feces as a normal part of their jobs; packinghouse and cannery workers, who must keep up with the pace of the line, standing on slippery floors next to workers wielding sharp knives. Fellow Worker Chumley would find little distance between his world and that of our 21st century.

Jack Sheridan's "Breakfast with Destiny" columns from the *Industrial Worker* in 1959 engage the key issues of today's anti-corporate globalization movement. Far from seeking to promote localism, provincialism, or protectionism, Sheridan uses the constituent elements of our early morning lives—the bed from which we rise, the coffee we drink, the sugar we stir into our coffee, the food we eat, the paper on which is printed the newspapers we read—to remind us of the interconnectedness of work and workers throughout the world. Our breakfasts have come to us from all over the world, made by workers in a variety of industrial structures (from slavery to wage labor), and they are shipped to us through a variety of economic systems (from colonialism to free trade). Sheridan's mode of argumentation is quite different from T-Bone Slim's, but it is just as effective.

Sheridan distinguishes himself as a materialist philosopher, finding the meanings and implications in the small details of everyday life. "Breakfast is commonplace and we take it for granted as an everyday occurrence in our lives and think nothing of it," he writes. "Yet as an item of culture it outweighs all the sermons that have ever been preached."[22] Sheridan wants to wake us up, as consumers at the final end of the food chain, to increase our awareness of these processes and these workers, not so that we can opt for a life of pristine simplicity, but so that we can connect with these workers and, together, shape the world, intentionally, in our own image. At the conclusion of his series, he writes:

> Man has made history and, taken by and large, it has been bad history; it has been history making by impulse, history making without sufficient forethought, history making without plan or purpose, and, to make matters worse, man in his making of history has selected and worked with ideas which, by the way, are the poorest material in the world to work with. If someone would, or could, work out a plan by which everybody could have

> a first class breakfast every morning, we would have a real start in the making of a human world.

In his article, "R-R-R-Raw Food!," veteran Wobbly hobo poet, Bughouse Square denizen, and lover of the outdoors, Jim Seymour, makes a plea for vegetarianism—and more—that would warm the cockles of the heart of today's college students and food co-op activists. "Murder is murder," he writes, "regardless of the number of feet possessed by the murdered creature."[23] In his essay included in this collection, Seymour argues not just against the consumption of meat but makes an impassioned case for raw food. He demonstrates that Wobbly activists looked at the food industry as more than a place to earn a wage (high or low), but as a place to nourish the mind and the spirit as well as the body. Like L.S. Chumley, T-Bone Slim, and Jack Sheridan—the other writers/ activists in this volume—Fellow Worker Seymour provides a vision of revolutionary unionism that includes new ways of looking at and organizing everyday life.

The materials—pamphlets, poetry, and newspaper columns—collected in this volume offer today's workers a first class breakfast, a place to begin consideration of all our places in the food chain, from farming to processing and production to the preparation and serving of meals. The metaphor reminds us of the ways that workers and consumers are bound in their work and by their most fundamental of bodily practices—eating—by broad economic and social decisions from which workers' input has been excluded. We are bound by these chains of the food industry.

T-Bone Slim, L.S. Chumley, Jack Sheridan, and Jim Seymour offer us acute analyses of these industries and processes, and, even more importantly, they offer us access to the IWW vision of how to break these chains, how to change the world. This liberating vision, nurtured for generations by working men and women like the four to whom we are listening here, has never been the sole property of the IWW itself, and it is up to us to decide how to use it on our own behalf.

St Paul, 2004

NOTES

1. Eric Schlosser, *Fast Food Nation* (NY: Houghton Mifflin, 2001), pp. 68-69.

2. "Building Blue Collar ... Burgers?" CBSNEWS.com, Feb. 20, 2004; *Fast Food Nation*, p. 73.

3. *Fast Food Nation*, p. 73. Also, Ester Reiter, *Making Fast Food: From the Frying Pan into the Fryer* (Montreal: McGill-Queen's University Press, 1991), and Robin Leidner, *Fast Food, Fast Talk: Service Work and the Routinization of Everyday Life* (Berkeley: University of California Press, 1993).

4. Robin D.G. Kelley, *Race Rebels: Culture, Politics, and the Black Working Class* (NY: Free Press, 1994), pp. 1-2.

5. *Ibid.*, p. 8. Kelley himself draws upon other scholars as well as his own experience. He cites James Scott, *Domination and the Arts of Resistance* (New Haven: Yale University Press, 1990) and *Weapons of the Weak: Everyday Forms of Peasant Resistance* (New Haven: Yale University Press, 1985). Also, E.P. Thompson, *The Making of the English Working Class* (NY: Vintage, 1963); David Montgomery, *Workers' Control in America: Studies in the History of Work, Technology, and Labor Struggles* (Cambridge: Cambridge University Press, 1979).

6. Carter Goodrich, *The Frontier of Control* (London: Pluto Press, 1975) and *The Miner's Freedom* (NY: Arno, 1977), both originally published in the 1920s.

7. Dorothy Sue Cobble, *Dishing It Out: Waitresses and Their Unions in the Twentieth Century* (Urbana: University of Illinois Press, 1991), especially Part I: "The Occupational Community of Waitressing." On emotional labor, see Arlie Hochschild, *The Managed Heart: The Commercialization of Human Feeling* (Berkeley: University of California Press, 1983. For a contemporary critique of mass-produced food products, see the popular 2004 documentary, "Super Size Me," by Morgan Spurlock.

8. Cobble, *ibid.*, chapter 3: "The Emergence and Survival of Waitress Unionism"; James R. Barrett, *Work and Community in the Jungle: Chicago's Packinghouse Workers, 1894-1922* (Urbana: University of Illinois Press, 1990); Philip S. Foner, *History of the Labor Movement in the United States, Volume II: From the Founding of the American Federation of Labor to the Emergence of American Imperialism* (NY: International Publishers, 1955); *Volume III: The Policies and Practices of the American Federation of Labor, 1900-1909* (NY: International Publishers, 1964); *Volume V: The AFL in the Progressive Era, 1910-1915* (NY: International Publishers, 1980).

9. Salvatore Salerno, *Red November, Black November: Culture and Community in the Industrial Workers of the World* (Albany: State University of New York Press, 1989); Salvatore Salerno, ed., *Direct Action & Sabotage: Three Classic IWW Pamphlets from the 1910s* (Chicago: Charles H. Kerr, 1997). The pamphlets are William Trautman, "Direct Action and Sabotage" [1913], Walker C. Smith, "Sabotage: Its History, Philosophy, and Function" [1913], and Elizabeth Gurley

Flynn, "Sabotage: The Conscious Withdrawal of the Workers' Industrial Efficiency" [1916]. More IWW pamphlets from this period can be found at www.workerseducation.org/crutch. Other materials from the IWW's history can be found in Joyce Kornbluh, ed., *Rebel Voices: An IWW Anthology* (Chicago: Charles H. Kerr, 1988). See also Frank Tobias Higbie, *Indispensable Outcasts: Hobo Workers and Community in the American Midwest, 1880-1930* (Urbana: University of Illinois Press, 2003); Mike Davis, "The Stop Watch and the Wooden Shoe: Scientific Management and the Industrial Workers of the World," in James Green, ed., *Workers' Struggles, Past and Present* (Philadelphia: Temple University Press, 1983).

10. Stewart Bird, Dan Georgakas, and Deborah Shaffer, eds., *Solidarity Forever: An Oral History of the IWW* (Chicago: Lakeview Press, 1985); William D. Haywood, *With Drops of Blood the History of the IWW Has Been Written* [1917], available at www.workerseducation.org/crutch.. Information on the IWW's contemporary activities can be found at the above website, maintained by Jim Crutchfield of the New York IWW, and www. iww.org.

11. David Montgomery, "The New Unionism and the Transformation of Workers' Consciousness in America", in *Workers' Control in America, op.cit.* ; Len DeCaux, *Labor Radical: From the Wobblies to the CIO* (Boston: Beacon Press, 1970); Al Richmond, *A Long View From the Left* (NY: Houghton Mifflin, 1972); Alice and Staughton Lynd, eds., *Rank and File: Personal Histories by Working Class Organizers* (Boston; Beacon Press, 1973); James R. Barrett, *William Z. Foster and the Tragedy of American Radicalism* (Urbana: University of Illinois Press, 2002).

12. L.S. Chumley, *Hotel, Restaurant, and Domestic Workers: How They Work and How They Live* (Chicago: IWW, 1918), reprinted in this collection.

13. Chumley, *op.cit.*; Frank Bohn, "The Strike of the New York Hotel and Restaurant Workers," *International Socialist Review* 13 (February 1913); Louis Melis, "Hotel, Restaurant, and Domestic Workers," *Industrial Worker*, April 1919. There are other documents available in the IWW Collection at the Walter Reuther Archives at Wayne State University in Detroit. Melvyn Dubofsky, *When Workers Organize: New York in the Progressive Era* (Amherst: University of Massachusetts Press, 1968), pp. 120-125; Matthew Josephson, *Union House, Union Bar: The History of the Hotel and Restaurant Employees' and Bartenders' International Union, AFL-CIO* (NY: Hotel Employees and Restaurant Employees' International Union, 1956).

14. Cobble, *op.cit*, Part II: "Waitresses Turn to Economic and Political Organization"; Nancy Schrom Dye, *As Equals, As Sisters: Feminism, The Labor Movement, and the Women's Trade Union League* (NY: Columbia University Press, 1980); Karl Korstad, "Black and White Together: Organizing the South with the Food, Tobacco, Agricultural & Allied Workers' Union (FTA-CIO), 1946-1952, in Steve Rosswurm, ed., *The CIO's Left-Led Unions* (New Brunswick, N.J.: Rutgers University Press, 1992); Roger Horowitz, *"Negro and White, United and Fight": A Social History of Industrial Unionism in Meatpacking, 1930-1990*

(Urbana: University of Illinois Press, 1997); Rick Halpern, *Down on the Killing Floor: Black and White Workers in Chicago's Packinghouses, 1904-1954* (Urbana: University of Illinois Press, 1997); Don Mitchell, *The Lie of the Land: Migrant Workers and the California Landscape* (Minneapolis: University of Minnesota Press, 1996); Vicki Ruiz, *Cannery Women, Cannery Lives: Mexican Women, Unionization, and the California Food Processing Industry* (Albuquerque: University of New Mexico Press, 1987); Denis Valdes, *Al Norte: Agricultural Workers in the Great Lakes Region, 1917-1970* (Austin: University of Texas Press, 1991); Ronald Takaki, *Strangers From a Different Shore: A History of Asian-Americans* (NY: Penguin, 1989); Linda C. Majka and Theo Majka, *Farmworkers, Agribusiness, and the State* (Philadelphia: Temple University Press, 1982).

15. On the 1960s IWW resurgence see Franklin Rosemont and Charles Radcliffe, eds., *Dancin' in the Streets: Anarchists, IWWs, Surrealists, Situationists & Provos in the 1960s as Recorded in the Pages of* The Rebel Worker & Heatwave (Chicago: Charles H. Kerr, 2005). See also Fred Thompson and Patrick Murfin, *The IWW: Its First Seventy Years* (Chicago: IWW, 1977). More details on IWW food-industry organizing in those years can be found in *The Rebel Worker* 1 (1964), p, 5; *The Rebel Worker* 2 (1964), p. 5; and in Torvald Faegre, "Organizing Blueberries," *ibid.*, pp. 6-9. On the San Francisco coffee-house strike, see *The Rebel Worker* 3, p. 3. See also Eugene Nelson, *Huelga: The First Hundred Days of the Great Delano Grape Strike* (Delano: Farm Workers Press, 1966).

16. On the Coca-Cola campaign, see the website www.killercoke.org.On the Starbucks story, see Derek Seidman, "Starbucks Workers Get Organized," www.counterpunch.org/seidman08262004.html; also, see the following websites: www.iww.org/union/iu660/starbucks; www.retailworker.com

17. On the Independent Union of All Workers, see Peter Rachleff, *Hard-Pressed in the Heartland: The Hormel Strike and the Future of the Labor Movement* (Boston: South End Press, 1993), chapter 2, "P-9's Militant Predecessor." I have analyzed the IUAW experience through a variety of lenses in several essays: "Organizing 'Wall-to-Wall': The Independent Union of All Workers, 1933-1937," in Staughton Lynd, ed., *"We Are All Leaders": The Alternative Unionism of the Early 1930s* (Urbana: University of Illinois Press, 1996); "The Failure of Minnesota Farmer-Laborism," in Kevin Boyle, ed., *Organized Labor and American Politics, 1894-1994* (Albany: State University of New York Press, 1994); and "Turning Points in the Labor Movement: Three Key Conflicts," in Clifford Clark, ed., *A Century of Change: The State and Its People Since 1900* (St. Paul: Minnesota Historical Society Press, 1990).

18. Ray M. Tillman and Michael S. Cummings, eds., *The Transformation of U.S. Unions* (Boulder, Colorado: Lynne Reiner Publishers, 1999); Ellen Meiksins Wood, Peter Meiksins, and Michael Yates, eds., *Rising From the Ashes? Labor in the Age of "Global Capitalism"* (NY: Monthly Review Press, 1998); Bruce Nissen, ed., *Which Direction for Organized Labor?* (Detroit: Wayne State University Press, 1999); Lowell Turner, Harry Katz, and Richard Hurd, eds., *Rekindling the Movement: Labor's Quest for Relevance in the 21st Century*

(Ithaca: Cornell University Press, 2001).

19. The most useful place to begin to understand the history of racism in the making and re-making of the U.S. working class is David Roediger, *The Wages of Whiteness* (NY: Verso, 1991).

20. T-Bone Slim, *Starving Amidst Too Much, Including Poets and Pearls and Recipes for Health* (Chicago: IWW, n.d.[1923]), reprinted in this collection.

21. L.S. Chumley, *Hotel, Restaurant, and Domestic Workers: How They Work and How They Live* (Chicago: IWW, 1918), reprinted in this collection.

22. Jack Sheridan, "Breakfast with Destiny," a series of columns from *Industrial Worker*, October 19, 1959, November 2, 1959, November 16, 1959, November 30, 1959, reprinted in this collection.

23. Jim Seymour, "R-R-R-Raw Food!" in *The New Justice* I:13, (Los Angeles, August 15, 1919), p. 13, reprinted in this collection.

CAPITALIST, handing the Unemployed a cup of coffee and a sandwich: *"Why, man, I don't want to see you starve—I need you to keep my employees from asking higher wages."* (cartoon by Art Young)

Mike Konopacki: T-Bone Slim postcard (1992)

T-BONE SLIM

Starving Amidst Too Much

Including *Poets and Pearls:* A Rhapsody
& *Recipes for Health* (Scientific)

Poets and Pearls

Our poet came near landing another job today. He was walking along the street, wondering where he could raise the price of a Turkish Bath to match his cleanly raiment, when his eyes lit upon a sign:

"*Dishwasher Wanted, Experienced.*"

Dear Reader: let me interrupt you while I tell you I can see the Editor's eye gleam *bale*fully, as he anticipates the harrowing tale of his crack poet cracking dishes.

He will rise up in his sanctum, paw the air and distribute hands full of hair in the wastebasket—the mere thought of our poet entering the "field of art"—Spasms of suppressed Emotion will shake his frame and he will utter words no Mule Skinner need be ashamed of, even though the Editor may repent, and deny them later.

He will try to argue that a premier poet, with fine spelling and comprehensive punctuation, is frittering away his time diving for pearls, in a restaurant, when he might be making himself useful wheeling sonnets on a Construction Job.

But our poet will cite authorities to prove that former great poets have reached dizzy heights in the fertile plains of Art, on the verdant pastures of Science.

Robert Burns, the brilliantmost star in poesy's constellation, won greater fame as a wielder of the broom than our modest bard can hope to ever win—washing dishes.

"Dishwasher Wanted, Exp."

Here was my opportunity for a Turkish bath. Our poet might enter the sweat-box kitchen, perspire to his hide's content, and get paid for it. Wash six thousand dishes for pastime, scrub the floor, compliment the cook, and while away the rest of the day discussing relative merits of chewing gum as essence piquant added to soup, with or without celery.

All this for $1.42, six to seven hours per day, and bath; and coffee, and beans, and comebacks and never-arriveds, etc.

I entered—in my best voice, and choice words, I informed the proprietor that his anxieties, from this moment on, would be banished; that I, even I, the inimitable immaculate T-Bone Slim, had resolved to emancipate him from the drudgery of the sink; that I would undertake to bathe his superb china (in the sweet water of Lake Minnetonka, if necessary), to maintain the spotless purity of the "hot-dog" joint, Le Par Excellence—would he kindly reveal to me the nature of the wages I would be honor'd with?

"Certainly, my friend," (I had won a friend already—though I hadn't touched the dishes). "Certainly," he says, "we are paying ten dollars a week and we furnish all the soap and water..."

"Why damn it, man, you don't want an *expert* dishwasher—what you want is a *common* dishwasher"—I had reverted back to my mother tongue.

"Are you an experienced man?" he inquired.

"Why man alive," say I, "I've cracked rock on some of the leading rock piles all over the country." (This, of course, was a lie.) Little indeed "moots" a lie when facing the realities of life; when a man wants a job, and a good sweat over a tank of dishes, little, indeed.

"Well if that's the case," he says, "I'll give you Eleven dollars and a quarter."

"What in the name of benevolence is the quarter for?" I inquired.—"Make it Eighteen dollars a week and free pie three times a day—I'll take it."

" Goodness Gracious," he exclaimed, "Eighteen dollars a week—that would be seventy-seven dollars a month; eight hundred dollars a year. Eight hundred dollars, just think—

"With eight hundred dollars you would be able to support a family. No, no, this place cannot afford to support a family, excepting, of course, my own dear family—leave me," he pleaded, "We—we couldn't afford to let you eat any custard pie anyway. Good Day," he says, as he hit me in the eye with a fresh doughnut.

With my remaining eye I saw that if I prolonged the conference he would still hang on to his money (but lose his mind) so I went (as is a custom with great poets) down to the river—but not to drown myself—I'll get a chance to wash dishes yet—when the weather gets warmer.

Cover of the Spanish-language edition
of the IWW's famous pamphlet, *One Big Union*

Foreword

What would you think of a son who would steal the best piece of meat from his poor old father who had been working hard all day—a great big husky good-for-nothing son I mean? You'd feel like knocking a "branch" off him, wouldn't you? Now wouldn't you? I'm afraid you would. Well, Mr Labor, you have such a son. His name is Capitalism.

He eats all the good things from your table and leaves you the "scraps." How does he get by with it? I will tell you. This unnatural child is the son of a widow, "Business," whom you married. She is in "cahoots" with her son and they are both "beating" you to it. Why don't you turn 'em "both" out of the house!

Now I don't like to butt into family affairs. So, I won't go into details to show how Business sends all our good things to your neighbor, Europe—I will merely give you a tip: turn them both out —and get yourself a divorce.

"A word to the wise is sufficient."

APOLOGY NO. 2

No man can write a book "on this Industry"—He may cover the book but he cannot cover the subject.

Our best effort is only a little more than Nothing. The author has been starved mentally, physically and—Powerfully. Hence, the name of the thing is *Starving Amidst Too Much*—Let's go!

An IWW "Silent Agitator" Sticker

PART I

PUTTING THE "KICK" IN, BY TAKING "IT" OUT

The present day managers of the food industry are self appointed. They like to point to themselves as "self made."—We won't argue that point.

We will not even discuss the terrible botch they have made of the job, unless it is to touch upon it in a perfunctory manner, now and again, when we wish to work up a peeve or to give our literary style a work-out.

Far be it from us to say they are ignorant—that they are all ignorant. No, we do not say so, but it would surprise you the amount of ignorance that is contained in that small and select tribe that dictate what we shall eat—and when.

Is it a part of wisdom to preserve our food with poisons? Is it a part of intelligence to squeeze the juice out of meats, and feed the pulp to workers? Is it sound logic to separate the small good (the juice), from the mass of bad (the pulp), and feed the pure good (the juice), to the few; the pure bad (the pulp,), to the many? According to my way of thinking these two should be inseparable.

Such is not the case, however. The juice is sold at a fancy figure, as beef extracts and bouillon cubes; the pulp is delivered, at more modest prices under various guises. This, foregoing, is given only as a sample of their shortsighted policy—They are emphasizing the "classes" that exist, and the struggle that persists between the few who enjoy, and the many whom they employ.

But it is not our funeral. Let them go ahead in their profound ignorance. Let them garner unto themselves all the good things of life. Let them hog the "right of way" to wealth, health, and happiness; then let us see what will happen. If there is anything established in this neck of the woods, it is that Nature intended the juices of the meat to be eaten with the pulp. It never intended the juices for one man and the pulp for another. If it had intended it to be so it would have made bubbling springs of beef extract, for one, and mountains of pulp for the other.

However, Nature did not see fit to make such an arrangement. It joined the two together (in one animal). A complete food for man

(Vegetables even are "smothered" with germs).

To separate one from the other is to break nature's laws—to deprive one man of "roughage" and the other of "concentrates."

The one denied "roughage" becomes a degenerate and goes into the market for new glands; the other one, filled up on roughage, gets radical and begins to howl for a One Big Union. How simple it all is, when we sit down and reason it all out together. You can fool some of the people all of the time, all of the people most of the time, but you must not think that you can fool all of the people all of the time, and get by with it—any individual, or set, thinking so, will need more glands than all of the monkeys in the world are possessed with.

All of our troubles have the same source—the profit system. It is easy to understand: When too many profits go to the few, the many will become poor; and when the "few" who enjoy profits become too numerous, then the "many" must suffer a want for the very things which they produce. While it is true the bulk of wealth is going into fewer and fewer hands, we must not get the idea that the number of these who live from the work of others is growing smaller. No, if that was the case, time would soon solve our problem. Such is not the case, however, and therefore it is necessary for the workers to organize industrially, and to encourage the ever growing parasitic class to adopt some form of labor for a livelihood. Industrial Unionism is the only remedy for all the ills—the One Big Union of all Wage Workers.

THE OBJECTION

This accomplished, it would not take long to count the rest and decide whether we care to support so many. But there is an objection to industrial unionism! Time and again we have heard it from well-meaning workers: "We have been fooled so often that we are tired of unionism."

At first glance your objection seems to be good. *"You were fooled often."* (You must have trusted somebody. A man cannot very well be fooled unless he has placed reliance on some one. What was your idea in trusting the business of your unionism into other hands than your own? (The word '"unionism" doesn't mean organization chores). Why did you trust someone to settle your strike? Wasn't you feeling well enough to settle it yourself? Was you too sick to vote? You trust all your functions, as a union man, into hands that have been picked out by the boss, and then you come around bellyaching "that you've been fooled." You give your officials power to pull strikes, when the boss feels strong; to call off strikes, when the boss feels faint. You're a fine specimen to come around with the excuse that you've been fooled: Nobody has fooled you; you have fooled yourself. The boss has pointed out a union to you and he has said: "There's a likely looking union over there with pink ribbons tied to the chair-rungs of its worthy president" (by the way, the IWW hasn't got any president); you make a rush for the hall pointed out by the boss.

What! You don't believe what I'm telling you? Well I shall prove it!—The boss told you that the IWW is no good—You believe that, don't you? Certainly you do. How do you know that Industrial Unionism is no good if you have not tried it? Ah, the boss has told you in the press it is no good, and you have believed him—You have trusted him—You must be easy. (How's chances to carry your pay envelope home for you?) 'Tis just as logical.

Your objection to industrial unionism, on the grounds that you have been fooled too often, is no good.

The IWW does not ask you to trust it—it is not a faith organization. It gives you the best "unionism" at the least expense—it lets you decide everything by majority vote; it will guarantee the wages will go up faster than the cost of living; it signs no contracts with the boss to work; nor does it sign contracts to starve—in times of unemployment. Its officials are paid common wages, $4.00 per day; they hold office only one year at a time and must be at the point of production a year before they can hold the same office again. Our officials are workingmen—first and last and all of the time.

You have been fooled, and fooled, and fooled, as you say, and the time has now come when you cannot be fooled anymore. This is the time the Industrial Workers of the World has been waiting for. Your Education is complete. Industrial Union Number 460 can talk to you now.

FOOD

"When do we eat? Who's cooking there now? Where's the best place in town? Where do the railroad men eat? What the hell kind of a place is this?"—These are all live issues. All these remarks are familiar to everybody—I have no copyright on any of them. Food is vitally essential to life. If we can get food all else fades into insignificance.

Clothing and shelter are the external protection against cold and death, but food is the internal fuel and serves to keep the body warm and active. Impure food is the same to the body as sand is to the furnace.

Plenty of food is very healthy for a working man. There is no danger of overeating if the food is pure; if your stomach has not been previously ruined with improper foods. Food in the proper state needs hardly any chewing; and all the chewing in the world will not save you if you persist in eating the present-day adulterations.

A FULL MEAL IS THE BEST PREVENTATIVE FOR A BAD STOMACH

A half meal can be likened to a half shirt—it covers only part of the stomach; the empty part of the stomach is exposed to the gases arising above the food line; and becomes inflamed—this inflammation can be carried away only by poulticing it with pure foods, or by abstaining from food altogether; "coffee and" is the cause of most stomach trouble. Eat well; eat what you desire—only what you desire—and be sure it is of the best. That is the best advice ever given by one man to another.

Cheap meals are a cheap death—or a lingering sickness.

SLOWER LIVING

How to keep well has been told to those who still care to read the daily papers, and many of these articles have been the only ones worth reading. Doctors too have recognized the difficulty people are having in keeping out of a premature grave. Hence, I feel that it is no more than right that I should be allowed "to tell the world" how to keep well. I shall try to be more modest than some I know—so as to not offend those with finer sensibilities.

The only way to keep well (and you're sick) is to join the Industrial Workers of the World and do away with the foods that are making you sick; that is, making everybody sick; that is making the whole world "sick—and tired."

It will do you no good to shampoo your hair with rosewater or pine juice to stop your hair falling out, so long as the necessary pure food lies rotting on the ground—while you are tormenting your stomach with garbage that would overwhelm a buzzard. After a while (of this) you will need a complete observatory with the most modern telescope to find your shoes in the morning, if you continue eating the things the trusts are putting out—You are going blind; so am I.

IT ALL HINGES ON THE FOOD PROPOSITION

Our only hope lies in the organization of the Foodstuff Workers Industrial Union. Once't organized and in control of that industry we can declare an extra special memorial day and bury all the rotten food with all industrial honors. We can hire T-Bone Slim to preach at the funeral services—that is, if we can't get a professional sermonizer to officiate. We will keep on burying rotten foods as fast, and as long, as they make their appearance. And we feel that in time the pure, the good, and the fresh, will make its bow to a distressed world. And we will not have to write books on how to keep well.

Is the food that is served to the workers in the hotels, homes, and restaurants really fit to eat?

Unhesitatingly we say No. Under the Capitalist System of food distribution it is impossible to get pure, fresh foods for the home even, to say nothing about the hotels and restaurants. Regarding these from a sanitary point of view, our truthfulness compels us to say, the food is not fit; and consistently cannot be fit; so long as the profit system prevails in the foodstuff industry. Not that I blame the workers. In the hotels, restaurants, and camps everything is done according to orders.

The old sailors rule "obey orders if it breaks the owners" holds true in the foodstuff industry. Any unsanitary condition; *any condition of stinking filth prevailing there*, is due to the owners' greediness for profits.

Repeatedly the operating expenses are reduced and reduced until eventually filth reigns supreme. The workers therein employed have their health ruined and must periodically seek other employment; especially is this true of the cooks who are obliged to handle, in detail, the decaying articles of food given to them (to see what they can do with them). Beef steaks come to them sometimes strong enough to walk and it is then the cook must hurriedly toss them into a solution of vinegar, to guard his own health as well as that of the Board of Health (who are waiting to eat them). You betcha: The Board of Health knows about it, but what can they do?—The sacred system of profits decrees it.

I have worked side by side in a lumber yard with three A-No. 1 cooks who were trying to recover their health. Later I went into two of these camps and found the cooks' places had been refilled; in one, by an undertaker's assistant, in the other, by a former superintendent of a city garbage dump.

A real cook, though, comes nearer than anybody to making something from nothing. He, it is, that is the real scientist, doctor, artist and laborer all rolled up in an extraordinary piece of human machinery.

He has never received the support of labor, and still, day by day, he endeavors to do his best with the most damnable materials at hand. One thing I will emphasize in regards to the cook: The very nature of his employment is such that he must from time to time tackle outside work. He must leave his job or drop dead over a frying pan—This places him at the mercy of unscrupulous owners (in so far as his unionism is concerned). Under the present system it is necessary to have four times as many cooks, would-be cooks, and "meat burners," as would be required under a sane system—one bunch cooking, one bunch leaving and one bunch coming and one bunch working at other work.

The cooks are compelled to work eight to twelve to sixteen hours a day over a hot range that would put to shame a Scotch boiler on an ocean greyhound (on which the fireman work only four hours on and eight off). This plays out the cook in jig time and sends him far afield, sometimes, to gather a mouthful of fresh air—a sun bath. His unionism, and its co-relative, *solidarity,* suffers because of it. Which all makes it clear: only the one big union—industrial unionism—can shorten his day, lengthen his pay and take the stink out of the kitchen.

WHERE DO WE EAT?

The prices charged do not always determine the quality of the food: rather, the price determines *who shall eat it.* Almost always the quality determines the price; plus service; plus rejected food, etc. And it is entirely reasonable to believe that swill will not bring the same response from a customer as will a well balanced meal. But as I was saying, the prices determine who shall eat in these well ordered places—and there are many such.

These places are for the exclusive use of those people who are strangers to work, who are unacquainted with overalls and unfamiliar with the dignity of the "toil" that makes it possible for them to pay tribute to the profiteers of various high class hostelries.

And woe be unto you, Ye Workingmen, if you have the effrontery to enter these polished palaces—this is Democracy, "heavy on the mock." If you are not thrown out bodily, arrested as a suspicious person, your meal will come to you in a very abbreviated form, and your bill will be emphasized out of all proportion to the "crime" you have committed.

You're not wanted! You don't belong! As to the lower priced places, where working men are welcome, we must say the conditions are somewhat terrifying; almost unbelievable in this civilized age. Waiters rush to and fro as if life depended upon their ability to dodge around the tables and slide along the counter. A bedlam of orders vibrates the air—shorty-brown, "knee deep" or "three high," whatever the case may be, and your meal is slammed in front of you one-tenth done. Every trick in the trade is there. Every adulteration. Every imitation. Every substitution. Dare you argue that this is not industry—that the waitress or waiter is not an industrial worker?

Back in the kitchen, dishwashers (and other help) are sweating over their work, in 110 degrees of heat; to the detriment of their health, and the health of those whom they serve.

Never an artist painted a prettier picture than a clean plate—a clean plate with two smiling eggs on it, sunny-side up. Alas, this can never be (in the workingman's eating house), so long as dishwashers are under-paid, overworked and abused.

If it wasn't for the dishwasher, "black-plague" or hog-cholera would have us all wiped off the pay-roll by this time. We who feel above doing this necessary and sanitary work should be fed from a trough until such a time that we learn to appreciate the kindly modesty of a pearl diver. Let us all turn to help the dishwasher organize himself in such a way that he can compel the employer to furnish a well-ventilated, cool, sanitary place to work in.

The chefs, cooks, dishwashers and porters, have everything in common, and should be organized in the Foodstuff Workers Industrial Union, and thus identify themselves with the Industrial Workers of the World. We are the richest nation in the world —and in this connection I will say: *We can well afford to look after the welfare of our food care-takers!*

In the so-called better places, the life of a busboy is often times startled into a consciousness of filth that is mental more than material, and which seems to be an attribute of many a genteel guest. The pantry girl, on the other hand, associating more with the "help," is spared these mortifying moments. By all means let these children join the union of their class, to remake a world: to regain the "ideal" of a society fearfully squandered by abandoned gentlemen in their hours of wanton revelry:

But we have a glowing dream
of how fair this world will seem
When each man can live his life
secure and Free
When this earth is owned by labor
and there's Joy and peace for all—
In the Commonwealth of toil
that is to be.

—Ralph Chaplin

You who are reading this may not agree with me as to the cause of these evils pointed out. You may think that I have been rather harsh with the Capitalist system and that the cause for all this condition lies wholly, or in part, with the general slovenliness of the workers. But, if you so think, are you taking notice of the authority wielded, at present, by the proprietors, or owners of these places?

The Capitalist system even hasn't full authority to administer the remedy—the workers themselves have the authority. The Capitalist system of production and distribution has been in control (with the consent of the workers), and has permitted these things to go from bad to worse; the system's health boards are conscious of these things; but still these things remain.

It begins to look like a case of "if Nature won't, Pluto will." Verily I do believe they will have to organize a one big union before they can make an impression upon the boss.

But it has happened in the late years that working men have gotten into a habit of patronizing these better class places. Whether they are doing so as a matter of conscious understanding of the higher quality food to be obtained, or whether stomach-disturbance has driven them away from the common emporiums, is a matter I do not care to pass upon. Nevertheless it is true the workers have gone from one extreme to the other; from the soup line to the Waldorf-Astoria.

Despite the fact that every discouragement has been put in his way, we find the worker breaking into "society" to grab off a better meal at least once a year. His sojourn is necessarily short in these latter places because of the various ceremonies (accent on the monies) that are a part of these institutions.

Not only is it a question of money (which is mortifying), but the bill-of-fare is enough to discourage the most intrepid worker. While the food may be digestible enough, the bill-of-fare with its French-Latin terms is absolutely indigestible.

Here the question arises, what is the idea behind this un-American practice? Are the parasites that extensively patronize these places taking this method of securing a higher education? Are they familiarizing themselves with the French tongue (in these eating houses) to the end that they may be able to order themselves a meal in Gay Paree after things get too hot for 'em in this country? No, I don't think so—rather, I believe, the foreign tongue is used to tickle the vanity of a semi-simian-brainless dude and his open-faced consort, to insinuate to almighty labor that these dressed apes are superior beings; to cause a "1001 percent" workingman discomfort; to emphasize to labor that he is not wanted there.

Any other language would serve the same purpose. In true American language, "Tea" would be marked "Nebish," on the bill of fare; firewater would be marked "Skidewapo," and so on. The language used has no bearing on the food served. Chicken *á la King*, turkey *á la Flapper*, can be had at the "15 cents and up" eating houses. "*A la king*" translated means "like king." Hence when you have eaten chicken *á la king* in a cheap restaurant you become convinced that it was prepared from Tutankhamen himself or some other potentate of equal historic significance. Now the question arises: why does not labor eat in these better places?

It has here been hinted that money matters have a great influence upon man in the selection of a dining room. It also has been hinted that the French bill of fare sours the working man's stomach. Now it may be that both of these are the cause for his eating a poorer quality of food. You know there is such a thing as two causes for one evil. For instance, a corn on the foot may be caused by the shoe being too small for the foot; and also, it may be caused by the foot being too large for the shoe.

Let us examine the question of money as a "deterrent"—let us discover and see if the lack of money builds a wall around a freeman and tells him where to eat regardless of his inclinations. It's said that money makes the mare go. And it may be true. But the question is—does it tell the American workingman where to get off at? Does it tell him when to stop, when to look, and when to listen? Does money start and stop labor? Does it keep labor going and has it got labor on the run? These are the things I would discuss.

Our present-day society is so arranged that an employer sets the price on the only commodity labor has to sell; on the other hand merchants set the price on the things that labor must buy—truly labor is between the devil and the deep sea. The wages he receives determine absolutely his comings and goings. If the employer desires to deny him "the small luxuries," all he has to do is to deny him wages. This he can do at any time by denying him a job.

In this supposed-to-be-civilized age, a man supposed-to-be free, must get a permit to work—a permit to dig in the ground; a permit to delve here and shovel there. Some system! (A horse must get a permit to haul a load). This is the system the brain workers, supposed-to-be, are supporting. They are traitors to sanity.

A boss sets the wages when a court or judge doesn't; a merchant (and there are too many of them) sets the price on goods he sells to labor. Thus it would seem that labor has no voice—it must take what is given and it must give what is asked. The inequality of this has become apparent to Labor and he is organizing a one big union to set the price on his commodity.

Hereafter, employers, if they want to rent, hire or purchase labor (power), must pay the price set by labor. Labor is independent of capital; has lived without capital and can do so again. Time and again capital has denied labor a job—it has had the power to do it in the past and nothing has happened to weaken that power, up to date. It will do so again in a limited way—limited because it knows that to deprive "all labor" of the opportunity to earn a living is to court too sudden an ending to their glory—even for those who are accustomed to the best of everything.

SPECIALIZATION

Every thing is fast becoming specialized. And it seems a good deal "crazier" than it really is. For let us understand, specialization is the mother of efficiency. Efficiency, if directed into the proper channels, is a great help to mankind, but when directed to benefit those few who profit from the system, it is useless. Less efficiency would mean only less profits. For let it be understood: The master stands at a "pinnacle of profits;" the worker stands at the "level of living." *Between the "level of living" and the "pinnacle of profit" lies a stretch of unnecessary work, and the degree of efficiency or specialization practiced by the worker determines the amount of profits the master will receive.*

From this it can be seen, efficiency and specialization today is practiced for the sole purpose of increasing the profits of the few on top. But it is not so crazy an idea as it looks. It makes for speed rather than perfection. It makes for "not how good but how many." It divides and separates the workers, it takes away their trade and eventually leaves them "one turn of the wrist"—to do as long as they live. In that day the logical craft union would be the "Wrist-turners International," only there won't be any craft unionism in them days, because the workers will have seen that they each are a small part of a great industry and will have organized themselves industrially.

Specialization has already wrecked the craft and trade unions —although some people may not have noticed it.

In the beginning (for instance in the foodstuff industry) there were the cooks; they handled *all the food*, did all the baking: everything pertaining to the meal. They were the Cooks and organized a Cook's Union.

Specialization came into the kitchen. A baker withdrew from the cooks and organized a craft of their own. Specialization came again. The fry cook took out a charter in the "Half of Hell"— (I don't know how true this is).

A cook became a steward and withdrew from the Cooks. The cooks didn't strike often enough, so the second cooks organized themselves in a separate body. So did the dishwashers and so on. This isn't true of course, but it shows what specialization will do to a craft union. And shows what it can't do to an Industrial Union.

EXAMPLE

What will specialization do to the Pearl Divers' Union? Let us assume they have a craft union. In specialization: The Silver Polishers immediately withdraw and organize S.P. craft No. 1. The cut-glass handlers organize C.G. Craft No. 2. The pan scourers get together in P.S. Craft No. 3. The soup-bowl washers will light out for themselves in S.B.W. Craft No. 4, and so on; butter-chip renovators will want a B.C.R. Craft No. 5, and so on until there are sixteen standard dishwashers' unions in the big kitchens of the future. The plates will go down one chute to the Plate Purifiers' Craft Union No. 13, the cups will shoot down another hole to the Cup Baptisers' Union No. 7, and so it goes... That's what specialization is doing to the craft unions; tearing them apart. And that is what craft unionism is doing to the working class; tearing it apart.

In the foregoing I have intended no sarcasm—I am on the verge of hysterics because of my seriousness. I have intended to show that when the Plate Purifiers' Union No. 13 goes on strike, the guests at the hotel will be compelled to eat their ham and eggs off the fruit saucers. You see I figure the Fruit Saucers Rinsers', F.S.R. Craft No. 12, will not be striking at the same time—"The very idea!" they will say; "*Us* strike with No. 13? We should say *not*."

What must I say? What must I do? Must I utterly disgrace myself to convince people that craft unionism is doomed? Can I make myself more ridiculous than I am already—and if I do so, will it give weight to the message that I am trying to bring? I have done everything that I know—if I knew more I would do more. I have said all that I know—if I haven't said enough it's because I haven't the stuff, it's not in me. I have studied the industry mostly at the table.

Specialization has absolutely no effect upon Industrial Unionism. They can specialize and specialize—they can make every man, woman and child a specialist, still they will be industrial unionists.

Specialization itself is industrial—that is why it is so hard on craft autonomy.

HURRY

If we once admit the "Public" causes us to hurry then we must admit the Capitalist System is the Public. In the case of the Waiter and the Waitress we are inclined to think they are holding a "wrongful opinion" about the cause of their "rush." Why we should think so is more than I can say—we do not consider ourselves smarter in any way than is the average waiter or waitress— we imagine that an average waiter thinks that he or she is obliged to rush things because the public demands quick service. If that is the case, he or she is mistaken. The public has all kinds of time; so much so indeed, that on Sunday morning, when the system is "laying off him" he won't get up (out of bed) until noon. It is the system, the Capitalist System so called by courtesy, that is in a rush. The public can wait.

If profits drive the system and the system drives the public, is that justification for the Public to drive the waiters and waitresses? A halt must be called somewhere, and the waiters and waitresses may as well call it. They can do this best industrially—many of them have already said as much. Personally I recognize no public. I see only working men, and women, terribly driven by a ruthless profit-grabbing system.

HABITS

Sanitation is not a question of *enforcement*—neither is sobriety a question of prohibition. Men and women are not clean because of any rule issued by the board of health. Men and women are naturally clean; and if they are not, no amount of law can keep them clean. If men and women are filthy in their habits and surroundings, there is, in every case, a very good reason why they are so.

If a hotel or restaurant kitchen is filthy it indicates that the employees there are occupied with other work; and if it is filthy, the responsibility lies not with the workers, but with the employers. If it is filthy it is because the employer has failed to hire enough help (and what right has he to the name "employer" if he hesitates about hiring help at a critical moment?).

No, Fellow Workers, Man and Woman are sanitary to the extent that they can be under the present system of human servitude. A housewife doesn't need a health board to tell her to wash the floors ready for Sunday, to make the place sweet and cheerful for the husband on his day of rest. It is a labor of love that frequently tires her out so that she herself, out of temper, gets on the nerves of the hubby; and thus is destroyed all the peace and good will the clean home was to have established—sad, isn't it? Her work is such that this extra sanitation unfitted her as a companion to man. Man himself, more robust, and muscular, should stay at home on Saturday to take care of this extraordinary sanitation. (Think it over). Washing floors is the hardest work I have ever done (and I have unloaded fifty-three tons of coal in ten hours over the side). Think it over.

People are just as sanitary as they know how to be—nevertheless, at times, they are compelled to extra sanitation by law. But in most such cases an injustice happens—where the man has been moving heaven and earth, ten hours a day, to keep sufficient food on the table, and the woman has been busy taking care of the children, cooking, washing, patching, darning, etc., and then, when the health board comes around and issues orders to clean up the alley, the outraged man must sacrifice his rest, get a wheelbarrow, and work a part of the night doing sanitary work that the health board takes credit for. I say, that if this man and his woman had any kind of a show in this world, they would keep their surroundings neat and clean. But they have no show. They must be driven. These are driving days—whether you want to or not, you must.

The Capitalist system of production does all that lies in its power to prevent the citizen in his work of sanitation. The health board, appointed through the offices of the same system, make a periodical drive in order to be in position to claim credit (for the system; for our general all-around cleanliness).

But never do they interfere with the profits of business. Which shows their class consciousness.

The other day a wedding party in a big hotel, in a big city, was poisoned to death—never a big holler was raised by the big health board; and the hotel is doing big business, and no doubt preparing a big feast for the next big wedding party.

But the health board modestly takes the credit for all the sanitation brought about by the superhuman efforts of the workers, thus conveying the idea that if it wasn't for the health board we would be up to our neck in filth—whereas, with a "board," we are only ankle deep in it.

I could take any member of the health board into a restaurant, within a single car-fare of his office, buy him a meal and safely bet him nine dollars and ninety cents that he would not eat it. (A ten spot might be too big a temptation even for an officer to withstand). Still I hear workers saying "this and that" should be reported to the health board (every man, you know, feels that he is a natural born detective, that he has discovered something that the board has overlooked). Bless your heart! The board knows all about it—and yet, it takes the credit for our efforts. Is it possible they wish to convey the idea that the human being is less cleanly than the cat that buries its dung and goes through the motions of washing its face? Would they have us believe that a cat performs these sanitary moves because of some rule the health board has established; that a mule shakes himself and rolls in a carefully selected spot in order to conform with the sanitary rules, printed on sanitary paper, by a sanitary board? I am afraid that is what they want us to believe. But I am also afraid they will be disappointed.

We are living still in an age of reason and we know as workers that no sanitary board can bring sanitary conditions. We know that if we are to get a cleaner world to live in we must organize our selves into a one big union and compel the "interference" with our sanitary efforts to stop.

THE STAFF OF LIFE

In the giant bakeries we find the trust in control, and we find a great many improvements in the way things are done. It will not be necessary to describe the different processes because "these few words" would only emphasize what is pretty generally known; sufficient to say—the improvements in machinery, etc.—have not benefitted the workers to the extent that they have the millionaire owners. In fact the only change that has happened (that interests the bakery worker) is that he now turns out six times as many breads, pies and whatever the case may be.

The pie crusts are no longer rolled with a rolling pin or a beer bottle. A machine does that work a great deal faster; and the beauty of it is, it has practically done away with pay-day, and machines never kick. Great crusts resembling a calf's skin are now turned out by machinery and it would not surprise me much if they started turning out shoe leather the same way—about as tasty, with Trust flavor.

Every bit of credit for the improvements is due to the bakery worker, and he should profit by them, but doesn't. It is only the owner who profits. The worker still leaves his bed at four a.m., or four p.m., as the case may be, and works just as many hours—and draws just as much pay as before, yet his production is six times as great. Millionaire Ward modestly takes the credit for the vitovim loaf(?)—saying that his ambition has been fulfilled. (I wonder what he puts in it).

The tendency of today is to take this part of the food industry away from the people and put it into a few hands. Jobs have already been taken away and given to machines. So it is up to the workers whether they wish to lose out entirely, or organize with other workers of the foodstuff industry to get real benefits from machine production.

No credit is due the owner for the existence of the machine. He merely has "saved profits" from somebody's toil, and after an inventor has worked a week to drive through his thick skull the advantages in the machine, he has merely given the permit to have it put in; thus getting double production on the whole outlay. The bakery owner is a serious-minded person who knows his business so we will leave him considering Industrial Unionism and proceed to bottle up a few cases of cream or milk.

THE MILK INDUSTRY

The freedom of the workers in this industry is regulated by the speed of the machine. Much good tears have been splashed over the baby's milk. Hard-boiled newspapers have grown emotional whenever the milk was not delivered at the baby's door-step for any reason reprehensible, such as strikes for living wages, etc. If a belt conveying the milk in the bottling works slips, of if the worker grabbing the bottles from the belt, suddenly gets the cramps from drinking some of yesterday's milk, the newspapers go into a rage and denounce the whole layout in general, and the workers in particular. "The baby," they cry piteously, "think of the baby." Yes, these editorial reprobates do think of the baby, and that baby is the milk company.

In a milk bottling works, the greatest amount of efficiency possible prevails. Cleanliness is a rule well observed. But the interesting part is the speed of the workers in each operation. The maximum speed is required from each worker and the fewest workers possible are employed.

It is sound logic too, that when the many produce much, there will be more leisure for those who produce nothing. Ocean voyages are made possible for the parasites troubled with inland scurvy; trips to California—the parasite's paradise—are made possible by increasing the speed of the belt or by working the worker one minute overtime. That's how fast it counts up in industry. Driving the "trucks" to one extra trip a day makes life quite enjoyable to these silk-stockinged Dairy-men who eat in the Loop.

What does all this mad rush mean? I've just told you. It is not the worker gone crazy. No! He, or She, is as sane today as He, or She was, when He, or She worked sanely. They are driven to this mad pace by a cut-throat system of profit taking, and it is all for the purpose of keeping the worker down—down—down.

This mad pace is not necessary. We lived before with reasonable work—we should live with less work in connection with machinery, or we should be paid for it, which amounts to the same thing. If we received the full product of our toil we could retire at a reasonable age. This way, we retire when we drop.

THE BUTCHER

We hardly know what to say to console this necessary workman. Conditions in this trade have changed so much that we do not find him any more; we find only specialists. The nearest approach to a butcher is a "sticker." His specialty is "that" one operation, although, of course, he is able to do the other work along that line—if not quite as skillfully as the specialist is now doing it.

Strange to say, however, these specialists receive ordinary wages. The "former butcher" working on hams, for instance, is a specialist and does only a certain operation, depending a good deal upon the process prevailing in the plant. In one plant he will be paid six cents per ham, while in another he is paid two and one-half cents. Where he completes the ham in a single operation he gets six cents, but where he only removes the bone he gets two and one-half cents.

But the tendency in industry is to subdivide the work (and then subdivide it again), thus creating more specialists. The worker on hams, for instance, has reached the stage where one man removes the bones, one removes the skin and one does the wrapping. Each man is a specialist and being on piece work he works fast—he works feverishly—and makes a bare living.

The butcher who has learned his "trade" no longer has much use for it. Yet it helps him to "fit in" in any special position. Of course, I do not mean to say that he can do as fast work (right from the start) as the specialist did before him. No, that is not my argument. My argument is that specialization and piece work drives a man to act like a squirrel in a revolving cage—going like hell, arriving nowhere.

PART II

Packingtown

IN THE EMPIRE OF COLD STORAGE

Hogs and beeves are now stored like furniture for the possible use of some future day—or age. Sheep, fowl and fish also take their places in the frozen vaults of the packing trust. Everything in that line is preserved, reserved and conserved, until such a time as the people get ready to part with their hard earned cash, to still the hankering for a piece of fresh meat—which is in no way possible in this age of refrigeration.

A booklet of this description would not be complete if we did not pay our respects to the Packers in a few "choice cuts," as they are in the habit of saying. We will drag in an article printed in the *Industrial Solidarity*, the official publication of the Industrial Workers of the World. We will use it for a base and proceed to move on the works of the Packers Big Five: using everything but—the squeal of the hog.

MACHINERY AND ORGANIZATION: THE PRIME FACTORS IN THE PACKING INDUSTRY
(from *Industrial Solidarity*)

From the time when our forefathers used to tear down the primeval avenues in hot pursuit of the wild boar, to the day when hogs were raised on Arkansas farms speedy enough to outrun the fastest farmhand afflicted with foot trouble and designs upon the hog's life, is a long haul.

From the time when our blue-blooded ancestors outran and overhauled the Plebian boar, and sank their teeth into the struggling pork steak, to the day when a certain amount of red tape and civilized procedure is required to consummate the same laudable purpose (to consume the hog) is another long haul.

Civilization has done much to save the footsteps of the citizen of today. He no longer has to lie in ambush to pounce upon an unsuspecting razorback. He has *entrée* to the gilded cafes on the avenue where the hog waits in *state*, garnished with apple sauce for the delectation of the master mind.

Great credit is due the foodstuff worker for bringing order out of chaos and making it impossible for any man to lose out on pork chops simply because of the slowness of his feet. A legless man of today can participate in the ultimate disintegration or final obsequies of the hog—on a basis of equality plus—with the fastest runner in the world.

Now it may not be out of place for me to describe, in a modest way, the industry which has made possible the saving of so much shoe leather. The hogs, after they have grown ripe, are shipped to Chicago. Here, Armour, Swift and other leading citizens hold a reception for these travel worn, four-legged hogs, and considerable grunting is done by both factions.

Then the hogs are herded together in corrals, just like human beings in a street car—no more consideration is shown them than if they were tired workingmen trying to get home on one of Chicago's dilapidated vans.

A driver then takes charge of the hogs and drives them to a shackling pen, where four men, alternating in pairs, put shackles on them—this prevents them stepping on each other's toes—ah, if the street railway company would do the same to some of the heavyweights I have known.

The shackler then hooks the hog onto a wheel which carries it to an overhead rail along which the hog shimmies over to where the "sticker" stands, "ticket-punch" in hand—it is here the hog receives its transfer and hangs for all the world like a strap-hanger (but upside-down) and bleeds every bit as much—until dead.

(Reader will please note: The other night when I got off the Harlem/ Grand car, "a moving corral," my high-top Peters waterproof-shoe was full of blood, and it didn't come from a hog either—although I'm a hog for punishment.)

Let's see, what became of the hog we just now butchered? Oh, yes! Two men known as droppers drop the hog into a scalding-tub where they float like Ivory soap. Seven or eight scalders then employ themselves poking and pushing them under; for all the world like trying to drown a cork.

After the bath the hog is somewhat more presentable in appearance and one man proceeds to expose the cord in its hind leg (called cutting the cord), hooks it onto a chain which drags it through a scraping-machine (barbers, please note). The machine gives the hog a fairly neat shave and haircut, without any additional charge for a neck shave.

From there it goes to a rolling-bench (talk about your accommodations). The hog is in no position to appreciate this and therefore one man exposes, cuts the other cord, and adjusts the "gambling stick" (to keep its legs from chafing). The attention paid these hogs is really touching—ah, if the streetcar company only—but what's the use?

From the "rolling-bench" it is sent along on a "rail" onto a chain. Then a man with a gas-burner singes all hair left on sides and hams. Three ham-shavers put the finishing touch to that tonsorial part; and two side-shavers cover the "area" delegated to them. This is followed with a gas-burner operation on shoulders and heads; after which three shoulder-shavers turn their work over to a specialist or head-barber who ferrets out every last hair that may be hiding the vigilance of other skill.

Then follows another bath, a shower-bath; water squirting from both sides. How I envy them.

When the hog emerges from the shower-bath it has all the dignity in appearance of a Roman senator—and senators not so Roman, to boot.

Then in quick succession a hog-header takes all the joy out of the story, by skillfully unbuckling the head—this is called "unjointing"—leaving only a chunk of fat to hold it in its accustomed vicinity.

An inspector looks over the glands of the hog to find out if it has had discretion to avoid associating with grand opera, which is a disease prevalent among the various tribes of hogs—that never know when they've got enough.

Two hog-cutters rip Mr Hog open. Then two "snatchers" take out the guts—this is called "snatching-guts." A man who never has snatched guts cannot understand the deftness and cunning required in this work.

Three splitters divide the hog into two parts, lengthwise. "Headbench" takes the head, but the hog never stops. Two leaf-lard-pullers next take their share—one taking out the kidneys. By this time the hog's best friends wouldn't know him; and the hog retires into a "freezer" for a well-deserved rest.

After twenty-four hours the hog is brought forth "quite refreshed" and additional cutting is undertaken on the cutting floor—an endless chain carries it here. The nearly-severed parts are completely severed and dropped into a "rolling-bench." Two sawyers cut the bone between ham and loin. Ham is associated with loin—not eggs.

The men cut the hams off, then it is thrown on a block and a man with a cleaver chops the shoulder—shoulder goes down on the bench, sides down another. Four "scribers" saw through ribs on the southern border of the loins, leaving the belly part hanging on loin. Two "loin-pullers" pull off loins with a specially made loin knife. Two "ribbers" take out ribs. One man splits sides—separating back from belly. Belly goes through "rolling-machine," is flattened out—other bellies I know need it, too. Ho hum, one thing at a time, slaves. Don't rush me.

The belly-trimmers model the bacon, after which it goes into a pickle-cellar, is pickled and then smoked in a smoke-house. Everybody is happy except the slave.

Gentlemen, brothers, sisters and fellow workers: this is industry! *Slam-bang* Industry! *This is organization! Organization to get the most possible out of every man, woman and child working in a packing-plant. Organization down to the last officer who searches the workers at packingtown gate for fear the workers' wages are so low that they "might" steal a piece of meat.*

Organization?—You saw what happened to the hog, other hogs won't fare much better—pigs have a poor form of organization—it's all squeals and grunts. Let us organize an IWW among ourselves; between "you and me."

We need organization!!

What we need is organization enough to have the company searched to find out if it is carrying home any parts of our wages.

Let us take the IWW to work with us—T-B.S.

In the foregoing we have shown that not a flaw exists in the process of changing an animal into food. Nowhere in this process is there a hitch that could be blamed on the worker.

The worker has done his part only too well, with skill, speed and efficiency—and we have called this process organization. They are organized in a body which is called the "force" of the plant. They are organized by the company organizer—the boss—to do this work in such a way that the greatest amount of products (profits) possibly remain (after each day's work), to cheer the packing trust in its mad struggle for profits.

Where one man cannot keep up with the work in any part of the process, two men are put at it—this is done because any piling up of work at any point would make it easier for all those beyond that point. Also, where one man turns out more work than the next two men can handle, three men are stationed at that point.

The difference in the amount of work in one operation, compared to the amount in another, makes it necessary to have more men at one station than at another. For instance, one sticker could keep ten scalders busy. This arrangement makes what is called the speed-up system. It is organization—unfortunately it is also business—big business.

The speed-up system kills the man by killing his manhood. It seems to be a killing game all around. The seven scalders are growling because the sticker doesn't take his time. And so it goes all the way down the line, one bunch of men crowding another—and I'm sorry to say, sometimes one set of men will try to "burn out" another set of men. This is oxtail soup for Armour and clique.

But the sticker is not to blame for the amount of work he turns out for you to handle. He is only one man—you wouldn't expect one man to stand between you and a slave-driving system? The company knows how many animals he can stick in a day—if he turns out five animals less than the company desires, the company can fire him; there is nothing to stop it; you are not organized.

You have never had the power to tell the sticker how many animals you feel like handling. The sticker is only "a one man" in "one hundred and ten million people." He cannot fight your battles. While it makes no difference to him whether you handle one animal per minute, or one animal per hour, he must turn out the number demanded by the company. If he doesn't he won't last. You are working industrially and if you want to make your job a stepping stone to some of the good things of life you must organize yourself industrially in one union.

Every man in every packing plant must belong to one union only, before they can have peace, ease and comfort. And that union must be the Foodstuff Workers Industrial Union No. 460 of the IWW, I have said it—you have your opinion.

If the packinghouse workers were organized in the IWW no man would be fired without a damn good reason—unless the packers wanted a perfectly healthy strike on their works. No man would be compelled to do an abnormal amount of work.

You will notice that I have made no reference to the women working in this industry. I do not think that it is necessary because the women are quick to understand. They will know that I am talking about the form of slavery that dictates their lives for eight, ten and fourteen hours each day, in some cases not excluding Sunday. And when I say "man," they will know that I mean a "worker."

According to my ideas about the fitness of things, a man, woman or child working for a living is a "man" viz;—a horse is a horse whether it's male or female. Why should I make distinctions? Why indeed? Thus. The beautiful and gifted young ladies of the south-side slaughter-house are organizing themselves into a debutante organization of the feminine uplift circle, with the avowed purpose of coaxing Armour and Swift, etc., to contribute a few pennies extra into their forlorn pay-envelopes. No. I don't see them as misses; I see them only as workers doing work that would stagger a man. (But I do not see them getting a man's pay.)

That is why it is necessary for them to join with the men in this "drive" for equality. I want the ladies to be men for once in their lives— and join a regular he-man's organization.

A Mrs working in the packing-house is a man to me, a mother in a packing-plant is not a mother to me, a grandmother working there is not a grandmother to me. They are only men—unorganized, disorganized men. I will make no distinction. A bachelor in a packing plant is not a bachelor at all—he is merely one of the men who pay young Swift's fines.

PACKINGTOWN UNIONISM

In the first part of this "work" we have discussed the way in which juice is separated from the meat, leaving the "pulp," to be eaten by the many. And we have shown the dire consequences of such a procedure. Now, it would appear that workers are being so divided into several parts—into separate factions; and that it is in the interest of the employers to keep the workers so divided. We have noticed that the workers are divided into several "trade unions," we have seen them belonging to several craft unions hopelessly separated. We know that it is in the interest of the boss to have them so divided; hence we cannot but believe that they are divided purposely.

But the men who are doing the dividing, pretending to organize, tell us that it is impossible to bring the workers together. They say it is human nature that prevents labor organizing themselves into one big union; but the lie is given their words by the fact that human nature doesn't prevent them from organizing into groups of crafts.

If their "platitude" about human nature held true, then we would have to believe that everyone in any one craft union was of the same nature. We would be obliged to believe that one brother working in the boiler-room was unfitted by nature to belong to the same union with his brother working in the killing-floor.

They would have us believe that a man's work changes his nature to such a degree that it forever prevents him getting together with his fellow worker on the job to put an end to the exploitation of labor.

Previously labor had been divided by religion; previously labor had been divided by color; previously labor had been divided by language, nationality and race. None of these will work any longer. Never again!

Now they are divided into craft unions by slick organizers and the marvel of the thing is that the men—and women—stand for it.

It is given out that the question of "language" is a stumbling block which prevents the forming of one big union. And it is common knowledge that employers seem to think so—and it is for this reason that I undertake to discuss this phase of it personally.

I don't believe language has anything to do with unionism. We ourselves speak four different languages (sometimes all at the same time, when we get mad), still we are able to carry a red card. From this it would seem that the more language, the more unionism —but it isn't so.

Language has nothing to do with unionism, and the employer knows it. He knows that a man's nationality is no stumbling block in his way, when he wants to join with his fellow man to better his wages or conditions. The employer knows this. But he knows also that he is bankrupt for ideas how to continue to keep labor separated. Thus it is, we find his agents stirring up race hatred.

Some employers have a habit of mixing all nationalities together in "their plants." Now and then they advertise for some special nationality—this tickles those of that nationality and does the employer no harm. (I wish that I could explain this part fully —have no room in this book). After all the "languages" are in their place in the plant, the company's agents get busy among them; not to prevent them getting together but to convince them they cannot get together. The company is not protected by the differences of language. No, it has a far better protection—craft unionism. The company has no power except the power of the men themselves. If the men permit themselves to be separated into a dozen unions, it makes everything nice and comfortable for our Meat Barons and makes everything damn uncomfortable for the men. Take your pick. It's your move.

Separation is a bad thing. If there is any merit in unionism then the workers should belong to one union only. The idea of unionism is to unite workers; to strengthen them against the common enemy. If there was no enemy there would be no need for a union.

The idea of craft unionism is to get something for those only who work at a certain trade. They, of that form of unionism, also recognize the existence of an enemy or they would not organize. But they cannot get the full product of their toil with this form of unionism, because when they strike, nobody is striking with them; their strike amounts to only a much needed rest, and when they get through the boss gives them another contract to sign.

NATIONALITIES

While it is true that employers think up, with hired brains, many a shrewd scheme to keep labor divided on all questions that affect profits, and while they put many an obstacle in the way of unionism; nationality is not one of them. The employer knows, as well as you know and I know, that unionism is stronger numerically in the countries our labor comes from than it is in the country they have come to. They know that a foreigner is a union man by birth, whereas we in this country are just beginning to take up unionism. England has two times as many union men, with only one-third our population. If we were as well organized, we would have twenty-four million union men. We have only four and one-half million. Germany with half our population has twelve million union men. We have only four and one-half million. And so it goes.

Employers do not want foreigners because they "think them" less susceptible to unionism: no, they do not think so. They know that a foreigner that has the nerve to enter a strange land is of an independent spirit. They know that he has the same pioneer spirit that filled the original "fathers" who stubbed their toes on Plymouth Rock. (Our country is dotted with monuments to foreigners with exceptions, possibly, for Mr Sitting-Bull.) No, indeed. Nationality is not used to prevent labor organizing themselves; for the very simple reason that it can't be used. But I must tell you what it is used for. It is used to create speed tests between two or more nationalities.

Nationality can't be used to prevent labor organization, because the System drives men to organize whether they want to or not. *Nuff sed.*

To say that Nationality separates one group of workers from another is to say that a horse and a mule are not a team. Nevertheless, they *are* a team; and the only thing that separates them is the wagon tongue. If the driver pounds them on the back he cannot expect to prevent them organizing a runaway. And if they once start kicking over the dashboard—Goodnight, Driver! Of course that would be a very revolutionary thing to do. The team should swallow its oats (what few it gets), take its "hidings" (like a man), and "praise lord from whom all blessings flow."

Maybe this illustration is rather radical and maybe I should not use it. But the word "worker" surely must mean something. Doesn't the very word "worker" presuppose that there are those who do not work? How do they live?... If all were workers (and they should be) we would call them Men, not workers. What is a team? Answer: A team is a body of horses, entirely surrounded by harness, whose freedom has been taken away by man. The readers will forgive me when "they" understand I am (also) a freight handler and that vile men have loaded a 600 lb. oil barrel on my truck and I have hauled it, just like a horse, possibly with more intelligence.

INSPECTION

About a year ago we were reading in the press (that part of it that had not been properly subsidized) that "Federal inspection does not effect the smaller slaughter-houses"—that are nestling up against the big concerns. And it was stated, at that time, that the reason for not inspecting these smaller ones was: "because they are not in the interstate trade" or business.

From this it would appear that it is perfectly proper to sell diseased meat to people, providing the meat is not taken outside the state boundaries. It would seem that it is proper to sell the "natives" uninspected meats, while it is strictly improper to ship uninspected meats over a state border line.

What makes the border line so sacred it not evident. It is not quite clear why a law should be passed to keep the boundary line inviolate—why a "do not trespass" sign should be put up to protect our neighbors from our "questionable" products—nor is it clear why a law should be made to designate the boundaries within which rotten meats may be sold.

Each great packing-plant has, nestling by its side, a small insignificant "abattoir" where the native steaks and chops find their beginning. They are operated under "antique" methods; and "has-been" machinery is being used. Still they are able to compete in the "home markets" with the up-to-date packers.

Why is this so? Is it possible that the margin of profits received by the trusts is so broad that it permits the "independent" opportunities to make an "honest living" with his out-of-date methods and elementary machinery? Hard to believe.

The trust says that it is receiving "only reasonable profits." It is up to date in every respect, yet we find out-of-date firms doing business (in the same enclosure), year after year. How do they do it? The "Trust" products are inspected and, it is said, the "independents" are not. What does that mean ? Does it mean that if inspection of trust products would be done away with, the trust would be able to do away with the "independents?"—that is: if the trust was permitted to butcher its diseased cattle, etc., and sell its diseased meats? It would seem reasonable.

I do not know how far federal inspection goes but I believe it prevents the trust killing a sick cow or a sick horse. I believe that the trust would not kill an animal that is ill: and I believe "inspection" is only a formality that verifies it.

What the trust does with its sick ones outside of refusing to make meat of them is more than I can say—and it is not my place to say—let the trusts themselves get out literature to show the ultimate wind-up of a tubercular cow.

The prosperity of the "independents" shall also remain a mystery—but only because I have never been employed in one. If there is no law to govern the independent, in regards to inspection, I feel that a great injustice is being done our National Packers, as they call themselves. I believe that it is an insult to the packers, if a law by its structure, insinuates that "they only" need watching.

A CRY FOR MERCY

The National Packers (as they call themselves), are already piteously crying for help; although they haven't been hurt yet. Periodically, in the press, we find articles inspired by F. Edson White, the present President of Armour and Co., pleading justice for the meat barons—and will say that F. Edson isn't any slower than J. Ogden when it becomes favorable publicity for the meat packers.

But I think that he will have his work cut out for him in the near future. The farm bloc crowding on one side, the dissatisfied workers on the other; it would not surprise me in the least if the Trust should begin to sweat in the next six months.

A headline says, "F. Edson White Deplores Governmental Interference in the Operations of Nation's Industries." Well, I guess they *ought to be*, alright. But it would have been still more polite if he had said the "workers'" industries. Oh well, we can't get everything at once. At that, it is quite a concession when F. Edson admits that Armour and Co. own and control one of the "nation's" industries and that the government is interfering with its operation. "Only the feeble-minded would fight Business," he is quoted as saying. Christ! Is the government as bad off as that?

From his carefully worded article we can see that F. Edson is a strong-minded man. Everybody else is feeble-minded—which he was quick to notice. And the warning about the government is timely—although, of course, it takes a brave man to make such remarks about our government, even in peace times. Mr Armour would be doing a graceful deed if he would part with some of his exorbitant profits and give F. Edson an increase in wages: eighteen dollars a week is hardly enough for a man of his capabilities (that is the last published figure). "Yet," he declared, to the Association of Commerce at its luncheon at the Hotel La Salle this noon, "business is a target for a great many people who are the reverse of feeble-minded." Hurrah! The country is safe. There are strong minded people. Hurrah!

"But, unfortunately, they are using business for a target." Is it possible; can it be possible that they are not as strong-minded as F. Edson?

"There exists a class of short-sighted individuals"—(ah, weak-eyed individuals—then the "groups" have stronger vision: Thanks on behalf of the IWW), "who feel that they were created to combat anything that savors" (I've got you, Edson) "of business; and the bigger the business the more zeal they show in fighting it," he said.

I can't quite make out why Edson is kicking so long as only mental cripples and nearsighted individuals are using business as a punching bag.

"This bunch of zealots" (Are you having any trouble with harlots?) "have succeeded in making many people believe that big business is a thing to be feared."

Say, Edson, where's your kick? Isn't it better for your company if the people are afraid of it? But maybe the people do not fear big business. Maybe these zealots you speak of are telling the workers not to *fear* big business but *own* it.

F. Edson White is also a great short story teller. Here's the story: "Their procedure has been similar to that of the parents who point out a policeman to their small son and tell him if he isn't good the policeman will get him." (Now isn't that a shame—They should let the kid find it out for himself. Very Thoughtless!)

"Let them tell that often enough and the child begins to feel the policeman is a potential enemy and he grows up fearing and avoiding one who makes it his business to protect."

There's the story, Fellow Workers. If I could tell a story like that I'd quit writing and go soap-boxing. A bunch of Chicago kids avoiding a cop when they should be ganged around him for protection: That's what I call imagination. If ever Edson takes a notion to go on the stage he will be another Will Rogers.

We will let Mr F. Edson White finish his piece: "It is not so long since the government devoted much time, and spent thousands of the taxpayers' money" (taxpayers' money), "towards propaganda to restrict the national" (national) "packers in their operations" (operations). "They should have been earnestly trying to help the packers solve problems" (with taxpayers' money I s'pose).

"The experience of the meat packing industry is hardly different from that of any other big business. They all know the agitator who works through the government trying to stop industrial and commercial development."

There you have it, workers. F. Edson is kicking because some bloc-agitator has been trying to stop industrial development. Atta boy, Edson; Industrial development along the lines of Industrial Unionism, Hurray!

"More and more we are electing to govern us, individuals with avowed intents to place some particular class and its bloc in a position of advantage." (I wonder if he means the bankrupt farmers?) "The short-sightedness of this policy is manifest in the increasing number of laws calculated to hamper individual and business progress and to prevent outstanding commercial success such as we call big business." Quotations from *Chicago-American*.

Isn't that the truth, Mr White? You have said a mouthful! The National Packers should be allowed to make the laws.

It is common knowledge that butchers are best fitted for law making.

I understand your feelings perfectly, Mr F. E. W., and I know that you yourself wouldn't be a bad law-maker. I believe that you, Mr F. Edson White and I, Mr T-Bone Slim, would make an ideal pair of law-makers. And I'll give the nation a tip right here, if they want really cheap, durable laws, they had better see us first.

You yourself have given up a $70.00 job in Frisco to work for Armour and Co., for $18.00—you could throw off about eight more dollars. While I will work for the regular IWW scale—the full product of my toil. If I help you make a set of laws for this country, or any other country, I shall expect to keep half the laws that we make.

What do you think of my style, Mr White?

Yes, foodstuff workers, the meat trust is beginning to squeal —something serious has happened to it. Organize Now.

Note: The foregoing is material that I know should not be put so close to the Reading Matter and I only give it for what it is worth, to show the weapons used by big business to propagate the idea that they are pure and white—when they are sour and black.

Conclusion

Life, it is said, is a funny proposition. But I fail to see the humor of it. And if there is any humor in it, I would be sure to recognize it—for I have quite a rep for distinguishing the difference between the drab and the vivid. We cannot consider the business of life as an antic, a few years of clowning through the world, or as a farce that brings down the house of the future in outbursts of unroarious laughter. No, we cannot see it that way.

We see life, we feel life, as something mysteriously terrifying. We try to study it. We fear to study it. And sometimes when we are studying it we fear to step into it. We fear to put our foot into it. But thank goodness, we are not afraid to study Industrial Unionism, the breathing, living, protest of the millions against a system of wage slavery.

Although we do not know that we are slaves, although we only know that the alarm clock tells us when to wake from our sleep; although we only know that the hours are long and that the pay won't reach around; although we only know that a boss tells us that the company will do all the "sitting-down"—yet, we sometimes, somehow, feel that we are not free.

Adam, upon a time, felt that he was naked. And a voice said "who told you that you're naked." So it is with us: we don't know that we are slaves—we only feel that way. And the feeling is the strongest upon us in times of unemployment. We go from place to place blindly; asking, inquiring, if *there* is a job for us. We have felt that every man was against us. We have felt that every eye was on us when we got turned down. Where is the system of such proceedings?

Yes indeed, we have felt like slaves. No place is there a guarantee of a job. In a large country a man might travel indefinitely before he would find work. But as serious as is the lack of system in the way civilized people attempt to live, we find that the act of asking for a job has become very "matter of fact." A man will walk into the employment office; without tears or sobs he puts the question to the unemotional employer, and upon being refused he retires gracefully out to the street—to wear out more shoe leather.

Many a pair of high-heeled dancing slippers, too, have been worn out this way.

What is there about work that makes it so attractive? A gang of rough-necks will trample the weaker ones to death in their mad rush for a job. Do you call that a system, and is it the Capitalist System? Aren't you proud of it? Isn't it an elegant arrangement? So perfectly brainless; a child could invent a better one.

That is the reason that time is always pregnant with possibilities for labor. Society is practically "unsystematized." Everything seems to drift along in an haphazard manner. If it succeeds, the capitalist takes the credit; if it fails, the blame is put on labor. Hence, if we are to have the blame, we may as well have the game. If we are to be held responsible for the way they run things, we may as well have "a say-so" in how things shall be managed—or mismanaged.

We take the position that it is our work that makes industry possible—money and credit produce nothing. We produce everything. We produce money. We produce credit.

Nothing but blind folly can prevent labor establishing a semblance, at least, of a sane system of production; and the elimination of profiteering on the miseries of those who labor for a living.

Even the foolishness of these who would have labor depend on others than themselves for emancipation, partial or complete, can no longer stand in the way. Industrial Unionism, its benefits, will be made so plain that every worker will consider himself a traitor to himself if he neglects to enroll his name among those of his fellow workers—men and women.

An industrial union is an organization of labor formed in such a way that every man, woman and child working for wages, in an industry, can become a member of it. That means that they will not be divided in groups. *They will be* the group; the unit; or whatever you wish to call it. And "what they say, goes!"

When they are organized this way, they are the industry and they can regulate their affairs without outside assistance.

In the packing houses the workers have interests that need looking after. Their industry has built up a great concern; put Armour, Swift, et. al., on easy street, and put themselves in the alleys of misfortune.

It is up to them to build up a comprehensive and sensible system of unionism which would make a provision for every labor classification in the yards. Then, and then only, will they be able to voice their demands in such a way that they will get instantaneous attention from those gentlemen who now abuse their confidence. Things have been going from bad to worse, better to worse and back again, the last worse always worse than the one before it. It will get still worse.

Let us get busy. Let us discuss these things, in the yards, where the conditions are. Let every man point out to his fellow man the need for unionism. We are anxious to help and we cannot be too eager in times like these. We have everything behind us—our sad experience with craft unionism is the only black mark against our character.

It is not too late to get right.

The IWW is the only union that can live in an industry that is so utterly dominated by money power as is the packing business. An industrial union built by the workers will naturally belong to the workers and not to the packers—although the workers may later on decide to call themselves the packers.

For better conditions, for better pay, for shorter hours, let us organize from the "corral to the delivery" in the one big union. Everybody in one union—*and run that union.*

Throw your eye over the following clipping:

HE CALLS IWW "TRUE UNION."

Editor, *Daily News*: Unionism is the first step in economics, which is the business science built up through centuries of work by able men who understand the new conditions the world is facing. It is necessary if a union man is to count for the utmost that he should be prepared for his work by having material to work with. It is not evolution we are witnessing, but creation.

The broad vision that produces the event, facts, true unionism, is so alien to the ordinary A. F. of L. leader that it is rarely understood by the rank and file. Just think of its workers—blind leaders leading the blind.

If there is an answer to unionism outside of IWW, I would

like to find it.

The IWWs are the descendants of our revolutionary forefathers by choice. It stands for true Americanism.
—Fred'k Muller. —*San Francisco News*.

The organizing of the Foodstuff Workers' Industrial Union is the first sensible thing the world has done since the time capital started running things.

Recipes for Health

RULE ONE

A well-balanced diet of pure, wholesome food, properly cooked; pure, boiled "drinking-water," and fresh air (uncontaminated by odors of decaying matter.)

RULE TWO

Good clothes, preferably those not made of jute or tow lines—but you will need less and less clothes as you continue practicing Rule Number One.

RULE THREE

Sleep in a clean quiet room; but be careful not to fall asleep before you are in bed—it makes no difference which side of the bed you sleep on. Make sure the bedding is pure—the softer the better—and be sure the room is large and airy.

RULE FOUR

Do only such work as you like to do—if you don't like your job, quit (I mean: the nature of your work). Conditions can be made.

RULE FIVE

Do not remain standing too long at a stretch—a tired body multiplies weariness. Sit down frequently—the very act of sitting down is relaxation. A few minutes relaxation can undo the damage done by an hour of labor.

RULE SIX

Do not work too hard—a body only needs exercise. Hurry is unnatural—a form of insanity. A hurrying man is never in the full possession of his faculties. Example: A man hurrying from a mob trying to capture him cannot see, hear, or feel—he cannot tell afterwards, how he got away—all he knows is that he was "going some."

RULE SEVEN

Never tire yourself out—weariness is the body's protest against overexertion; against improper foods; against insufficient sleep (rest), against inadequate clothing. Weariness is a mild form of death.

RULE EIGHT

Always keep yourself fit to serve mankind. Watch yourself, do not watch the boss. Never exhaust yourself—there is nothing more disgusting than a man staggering home from work "dog-tired," helplessly falling into a chair to have his child remove his shoes; then grabbing a hasty feverish supper; saying good-night to his family and rolling into bed half-washed, to repeat the same thing three hundred and twelve times per-year, or until sickness puts a stop to his mad career.

IWW, n.d., [1923]

From Chumley's 1918 *Hotel and Restaurant Workers* pamphlet (cartoon by "Dust" Wallin)

PROFITEER: *"I'm as good a friend of labor as the next man—but there's no denying the fact that workingmen do spend their money foolishly."* (cartoon by Art Young)

L. S. CHUMLEY

Hotel, Restaurant & Domestic Workers:
How They Live & How They Work

Labor is on the threshold of the dawn of a new day. The rumblings of a social revolution can be heard in every section of the earth. In some countries, violent revolutions are in progress and in others, strikes are assuming such proportions that a world wide general strike seems almost inevitable. The workers are determined that pre-war conditions shall not prevail and are demanding actual control of industry.

Hotel and restaurant workers are by no means an unimportant group of the world's workers. They are, for the most part, essential and are destined to play an important role in the struggles between those who work and those who own.

In our everyday struggles with the owning class we can win through organization only. Individuals are wholly lost in the struggle. Craft organization is unable to meet the situation. It is only through the One Big Union of all industrial workers that we can beat the united bosses.

Of the hundreds of thousands of hotel and restaurant workers only a small part are organized and these belong to the Hotel, Restaurant and Domestic Workers Industrial Union of the IWW We do not consider the few who are divided into craft unions or bogus industrial unions as organized. The necessity of organizing is apparent to all.

Therefore it is the purpose of this pamphlet not only to arouse the workers to the necessity of action, but to suggest a plan of organization that will assure lasting results.

A number of papers are devoted to the report of the "Juvenile Protective Association of Chicago" on "The Girl Employed in Hotels and Restaurants." The report is sufficient as far as the women employees are concerned, but bear in mind that the condition of the men and boys employed in hotels and restaurants are equally as bad. It would take a book many times the size of this pamphlet to describe the abuses that hotel, restaurant workers and domestics are subjected to.

You will notice that I place hotel and restaurant workers with domestics. This is correct, as domestics are doing the same kind of work in private homes. They are domestics today and hotel or restaurant workers tomorrow, and vice versa. Their conditions and duties are about the same, therefore any organization of these workers will not be complete unless all are included.

More than ninety percent of the hotel and restaurant workers have been ignored by the A. F. of L. altogether. But if these workers were organized on craft union principles, they would soon whip each other to death, for this is one industry where craft unions have not and can not gain even partial success.

If we are to divide the workers into crafts we find that, in the average hotel where there are a hundred or more workers, there are from fifteen to twenty crafts represented. This would mean as many different craft unions. This would be dividing the workers, and that is what the masters desire.

The situation we find today is that a small portion of the "white waiters" are in a craft union: colored waiters, Greeks, and busboys are left out to become scabs in time of strike. About two percent of the cooks are in another craft union. Butchers, bakers, carpenters, bartenders, electricians, clerks, bellboys, checkers, dishwashers, maids, etc., are generally unorganized workers.

Solidarity has been a thing unknown to hotel and restaurant workers, consequently their conditions are about as bad as they could possibly be. The masters have taken advantage of this lack of solidarity and have brought about a situation that is deplorable. In the last few years wages have been cut, and in many places abolished altogether. In Chicago there are more than a hundred cafes that do not pay the waiters any wages; indeed in some of these places the waiter must pay to work. The work hours have been increased until eleven hours is considered by many a short day.

It has been said that "a waiter is a fellow who has tried every other line of business and failed." I heard a manager say that "waiters were a lot of thieves." The guests are not so particular what they call waiters, and some of the names wouldn't look well in print.

Webster says that "a waiter is a servant; a menial; engaged in servile work." And Webster is right.

No other occupation presents greater contrast among its followers than that of the waiter. Here the extremes are met.

Waiters as a whole receive very low wages, and yet a few manage to make more than the skilled worker. Generally the hours are very long, still some work only two or three hours a day. Some waiters are intelligent, while others are exceedingly dull, almost simple. Every nationality and race is represented amongst the waiters. Some waiters are fighters and are continually struggling for better conditions. Others, indeed too many, are pusillanimity personified. But we will consider the average and not the extremes.

There are said to be several classes of waiters. First, the waiters who work in the so-called "first class hotel and clubs" who get a very small wage, and tips. The honky-tonk waiters who depend altogether on tips. The park or beer garden waiter gets a percentage on his sales, and tips. Then there is the restaurant or eating house waiter who receives a wage and an occasional tip. Other waiters are known as "lunch counter wops," "beanery boas," "tourists," and the waiter who "wouldn't accept a tip" (this is a rare species). After all there isn't much difference—they are all servants, and their conditions are about the same everywhere.

They work long hours at an unpleasant occupation, the wages are low; they are ill-treated and abused. Waiters must be servile and humble. They are not treated like ordinary human beings. It is a common joke among waiters to repeat the newspaper account of a railroad wreck, printed a few years ago, it read, "there were seven people, two dogs, and a waiter killed."

Eleven hours is about the average work day for waiters, and including all classes of waiters, the average wage is about $2.00 per day.

In some places waiters work fourteen hours every day. In cafes and hotels, waiters get tips, and if they work hard and are lucky, they may make three or four dollars a day. But if you consider the hours, the physical labor, the foul air, ill-treatment, etc., the four dollars grows insignificant. Then the waiter must pay the busboy from fifty to seventy-five cents a day, a dime or two to the cooks, etc. He must buy some cigars or drinks for the floor-walker who seats the guest, and in some places he must contribute two or three dollars to the head waiters' "jelly-roll."

If a waiter's wardrobe is complete, it will have cost him at least one hundred dollars. His wardrobe, if complete, will consist of a full-dress tuxedo, regulation jackets, white vest, black pants, white suits, red vest, aprons, etc. Waiters also wear all kinds of uniforms of all colors, brass buttons, etc.

In nearly every case the waiter has to pay for everything he wears. Head waiters and managers take a keen delight in changing the livery of their waiters; they imagine it shows their cleverness. The "first-class waiters," the "aristocrats," have a club as near like their master's club as their finances will permit. The club sports an extensive bar, numerous pool-tables, card rooms where the retired waiters pass their time, and incidentally relieve the working waiters of their "hard-earned."

Head waiters, managers, and even proprietors may become honorary members of the club, that is, they get the benefit without having to pay for the upkeep. All subjects may be discussed in the club, except those pertaining to the working conditions and wages of waiters.

If you suggested that the club should demand better conditions, you will be told that the club is a social organization, and that agitators are not wanted in it. The waiter's club, like the Geneva A., is a place where the employers can get the best waiters, at the lowest wages. The club helps to keep a large supply on hand. These organizations are absolutely of no benefit to waiters, but they are of benefit to the employers. The busboy, being the assistant of the waiter, has a hard row to hoe. He is a servant to a servant.

THE TIPPING EVIL

The tipping-system is a product of evolution; it probably originated in chattel-slavery, as it is an ideal incentive for slaves. The tipping-system is a system of bribery that harms both the giver and receiver. It has the effect of making the giver arrogant, dictatorial, imperious, etc. And the receiver becomes servile, slavish, mealy-mouthed and beggarly. That is why it is customary to pay servants in tips because those are the qualities desired in servants. The rule is that those who depend on tips for a livelihood are slaves of the worst-type. No man with red-blood in his veins likes to grovel in the dust before people, who are his superior only in point of wealth.

There have been several attempts to abolish tips by law; at least several states have passed laws prohibiting the giving or taking of tips. Such laws will have about as much effect on the tipping-system as laws of like character have on prostitution. The tipping evil is certainly not a case for the law-makers, and cannot be settled in senate chambers. Questions of this kind can only be definitely settled by the workers themselves. Let us demand a wage equal to, if not more than, that made in our best day of tips.

THE VAMPIRE SYSTEM

The practice of head waiters, chefs, head-porters, housekeepers, head-bellmen, managers, stewards, etc., in demanding a fee from employees for the privilege of working, is appropriately called "The Vampire System." In more than fifty percent of the hotels and restaurants in Chicago this system is in vogue, and in many cases with the knowledge and consent of the proprietors.

The applicant for a job must not only pay for the job, but usually is compelled to pay regularly a part of his or her earnings to the boss. That this system is rapidly spreading throughout the country only accentuates the woeful lack of spirit amongst hotel workers.

Occasionally a head waiter or manager will agree to work without salary, if the proprietors permit them to exploit the workers under them.

Then an agreement will be made with an employment "shark" who will supply waiters, busboys, kitchen help, etc. The victim has to pay from $2.00 to $10.00 for a job, the money being divided between the "Vampire" and the "Shark." The victim is allowed to work long enough to get a fee to pay some other "shark," then an excuse will be made to discharge him. To get a job in some places you must meet the go-between or "fixer," who will collect the fee and take your name, then when you apply for work the head-waiter or manager will choose you out of the crowd, and everything appears to be on the square. Once in, you continue to pay for special privileges. Even the head bus and the head dishwasher use their position to rob the workers under them.

Many subterfuges are used to collect; there are suit-clubs, shirt-waist-clubs, raffle-contests, and all kinds of collections. The collector comes around regularly and you must contribute or face dismissal. Seldom is a reason given when a worker is discharged.

Another phase of "The Vampire System" is the custom of giving presents to the heads of departments. Barely does a month pass without a list being sent around to rob the workers. The excuses are birthdays, weddings, Xmas, etc. Perhaps a distant relative of the boss dies; around goes the list, every one must have his or her name on it or face consequences. Usually the list is started at the instigation of the boss himself; he also suggests the amount to be given.

How long are we going to allow these "vultures" to rob us?

THE FINING SYSTEM

The fining-system in hotels and restaurants is universal. The owners use it to rob their employees of part or all of the meager wage they promise to pay them. In many places, there are more than a hundred house laws. A fine is imposed for the breaking of any. And not one of these is justified by city, state, or national laws.

The fines range from five cents to the amount of wages paid. You may be fined for doing the thing that previously you were fined for not doing. It depends largely upon the maggoty-moods of your bosses. In one of the "Loop" cafes (Chicago) the auditor has the authority to impose a fine of fifty-cents or a dollar on any waiter who fails to return his blank checks after each meal. It all depends upon what mood the auditor happens to be in, whether it will be fifty-cents or a dollar.

You are fined for talking and for not talking; for smiling, and not smiling; for working slow, for working too fast; for making a noise, for not being servile. You are fined for not being able to understand the unintelligent order of an ignorant boss. You are fined for eating, drinking, smoking, etc. In fact you must ask permission to do anything and yet, you may be fined for asking. You are fined for sitting down, for reading a newspaper, for using the guest-toilet room, even though the "help's" toilet be out of order. You are fined for resenting an insult, for being late to work, and for leaving for home before you apologize to your boss for even thinking of home.

You are charged excessively for breakage. For breaking a dish that cost from five to twenty-cents, you are charged from fifty to a dollar. You are charged for the things the guests break or steal. In many places you must put up a security for the silver and glassware you use to serve the guest with. If for any reason it is not returned you forfeit the security.

Who gets the money that is filched from these slaves?

Most of this graft is divided between the managers, bookkeepers, etc. Managers explain that the fining-system is necessary for discipline. But that is a damned lie. They are thieves and grafters.

A waiter from Washington told me that he worked in a hotel where they had what they called a "gold-service." He accidentally broke one of a hundred cups, and was charged two dollars for it. The next day he very quietly broke the handles off of the remaining cups. No one but himself knew who did it. The waiter, who had left the city, wrote the owners that it was he who did it, and told them why. The result was that the fining-system in that house was abolished. This was his answer to this system of robbery.

WHAT WE EAT

Of course, you know that hotels, restaurants, and clubs feed their employees, and naturally one would suppose that the workers engaged in preparing and serving the finest of food would be well fed and satisfied at least as far as their food was concerned. Nothing could be farther from the truth. The average hotel restaurant and club feed their employees food that a humane person would not offer to a dog. In a great many places the scraps, refuse and "comebacks" are actually offered to the help to eat. In other places the cheapest-grade of meat, bread and coffee is used. I have tasted coffee served to the employees in some of our best hotels that would cause a strike if served to workers in a railroad construction camp.

Very often it happens that some of the help get sick from eating the food that is prepared for them, and I know of cases where death resulted. At one of the exclusive hotels on Michigan Avenue, Chicago, where the food is about the average, a number of the employees became violently ill from eating the food that was prepared for them. Several lingered near death for more than a week. One of the bolder workers began a suit for damages. The employers threatened any and all employees with immediate dismissal if they should testify that the food made them sick. The employees were bluffed, the case was dropped.

WHY WE GET SICK

Long hours of unpleasant work, non-nutritious food, and filthy locker-rooms are not conducive to good health. Consequently hotel and restaurant workers must suffer. These workers suffer from all kinds of diseases; the white-plague [tuberculosis] exacts a heavy toll. It is a fact that more than fifty percent of these workers are victims of this dreaded disease. This is not a far-fetched statement, their mode of living and working conditions make it inevitable. Consumption is a mighty serious thing, you can't fool with it. When the symptoms appear, the continual colds, loosing of flesh, a hectic fever, every minute counts. Fresh air is necessary: it does the curing, it is imperative that you live out of doors night and day. Eat plenty of fresh eggs, fresh beef, and drink sweet milk. Don't work hard, and don't worry. You must be comfortable and happy; then nature will cure you. No, I am not joking. I am telling you the simple truth, that your illness will grow unless you follow the above program. But how? Surely that is the question; how can anyone working in hotels and restaurants eat nutritious food, breathe fresh air, and not worry or work too hard?

The things we need most we get the least of. When you enter a hotel, cafe or club as a guest everything appears to be clean, sanitary, modern, etc. The marble is white, brass polished, linen is spotless. The guest rooms, their toilet, reception, library, gambling and sleeping rooms are perfect in every way. But how about the help, the servants who take care of these rooms and serve the masters who enjoy them? Here we find the opposite, just as with the food. The help's quarters, their dressing, locker, and toilet rooms are always located in some out of the way garret, a cellar, hole, or dungeon, that could not be utilized for any other purpose. In many places the toilet and lockers are in the same room. The toilet is seldom modern, little more than an open sewer. The smell from these places is nauseating. In such places, oft-times more than a hundred workers must dress and keep their clothes. The help's locker-room in the average hotel or restaurant is a menace to those who use it. And now laws are being proposed to throw out the sick workers from these places, not for our sake, but because sick servants endanger the master's health. They make no mention whatever of eradicating the causes of disease among these workers. At present it is cheaper to replace sick workers than it is to remedy conditions.

DISCIPLINE

There is only one other place that I know of where discipline is carried to the extent that it is amongst servants, and that is in the army. And the reason is the same and apparent in each case. The soldier's duty is not to question, but obey. He is trained to do things that are repulsive. Therefore it is necessary for the officers to domineer, bluff, and bulldoze the soldier. It makes him servile and obedient.

Hotel and restaurant owners, and their drivers, assume the same attitude.

Hotel workers are servants; they must be kept in their places, they must be obedient and servile; their duties are not pleasant, they are degrading. So the servants must be abused and bluffed, else they might revolt at some of the things they are told to do.

Waiters, busboys, bellboys, maids, etc., suffer most. Drunken and ill-mannered guests may, and do, abuse, ill-treat, and outrage these workers. And if they complain they are jeered at and told that they, being waiters, maids, etc., must overlook anything the guest might say or do. The manager, head-waiter, chef, etc., that cannot bluff his help lacks ability.

COOKS, ETC.

It requires as much intelligence, skill, and training to become a cook, baker, or butcher, as it does to become a carpenter, bricklayer, painter, etc., but a comparison of wages and hours should make the former blush with shame.

The average work-day of cooks, etc., is eleven hours, and the average wages is about two dollars and fifty-cents per day.

Think of a man working in front of a red hot range where the thermometer seldom drops below 100, from ten to fourteen hours a day.

Then consider the nature of the work, the skill required, the danger from hot grease, steam, etc., also the foul air, the wet floor, and general filth and unsanitary condition throughout the kitchen.

When I think of this, I wonder how any man would consent to work under such conditions.

Occasionally cooks, in different localities, organize a union of their craft, and go out on strikes, but immediately their places are filled by men and women whom the cooks would not take into their union. The sooner that cooks grasp the idea that if they are to get better conditions they must cooperate with the waiters, busboys, dishwashers, and in fact every one employed in the same industry, the sooner will they get results from their efforts.

Sometimes cooks get the club idea, and it has about the same effect as the waiter's club, namely, that of being beneficial to the boss and not the cooks.

THE GIRLS EMPLOYED IN HOTELS AND RESTAURANTS

The Juvenile Protective Association made an investigation of fifty hotels with a view of ascertaining the temptations which surround many of the young foreign girls who work in hotels, and the treatment accorded them by hotel-managers. The investigator visited:

13 first class,
16 second class,
9 third class, and
12 very low class hotels.

In all of these places the investigator endeavored to learn the conditions under which the girls worked, where they slept, what they ate, the wages they were paid, their hours of work and the temptations to which they were exposed.

It was found that in the first-class hotels the chamber maids were Irish and German, and in most of the low class hotels they were colored or Americans of the "down and out" type, but in all hotels the kitchen and laundry work was done by foreign girls, mostly Polish. These girls do not speak English and therefore cannot go into domestic service, but in hotels they are chosen for the following reasons: First because they come of strong peasant stock and accomplish a large amount of work. Second, they are very thorough in what they do. Third, they are willing to take very low wages. Fourth, they are very submissive—that is, they never protest. Fifth, they are ignorant of the laws of this country and are easily imposed upon. Sixth, they never "betray their superiors," no matter what they see.

The wages paid vary with the nature of the work. Chambermaids and expert ironers are paid the largest salaries, while the scrubwomen are paid the lowest. The first-class hotels, of course, pay the highest wages and the low-class the smallest. The highest wages paid a chambermaid in a first-class hotel amounted to $18.00 a month and the lowest $16.00 a month, both including board and lodging. In the low-class hotels the highest wages paid are $16.00 a month, and the lowest $14.00 a month, also including board and lodging. Without board and lodging the highest price paid to a chambermaid is $30.00 a month and the lowest $20.00 a month. The highest wages paid to a laundry or kitchen girl are $18.00 per month and the lowest $14.00 per month, both including board and lodging.

The hotel managers trouble themselves very little about the food and sleeping accommodations provided for their employees. In many hotels the food served is not only poor but unwholesome. In hotels the employees are obliged to eat the "comebacks" from the guests' meals. In others the food is served in such an unappetizing manner that the disgusted girls are not able to eat it. Many times they have no dining room and eat in storeroom or cellar. Of the fifty hotels visited only six provided good food for their employees. Eight fed them fairly well while in the other places no particular attention was paid to the quality of the food. The following reports are typical:

> The girl employees ate in a room just under the kitchen, which looked more like a storeroom than a dining room. It was directly opposite the boilers and the heat was intense. The room was dark and uninviting. The food was cold and poor. The tables were covered with old, greasy, blue oilcloth. The noise of the machinery, the dark entrance, and the lack of fresh air were enough to take away appetite.
>
> The dining room for the women employees was in a basement where odors of bygone meals mingled with the damp smell of the basement. Against the wall was a 'hang' table and down the center of the room was another long table covered with greasy oilcloth. Around the table were rough wooden benches. Here waitresses, chambermaids, scrubwomen, pantry girls and other women employees were supposed to eat. On the stove was a pot of stew continually boiling. There was a bowl of cold boiled potatoes on the table and a long ladle in the stew, to which the women helped themselves. One cup of black coffee was allowed to each woman.

The sleeping accommodations for the girls were most inadequate in the majority of the hotels visited. Weak and exhausted women, after a hard day's work, are crowded into poorly ventilated rooms. Most of these hotels violate the State Board of Health ordinance which requires 400 cubic feet of air for each occupant of a room. Many of the rooms assigned to these hotel employees never get any sunshine and very little light. A few have no windows. No wonder that in many cases the investigator described the girl employees as looking "as though they could never stand it all day," and added that "most of the girls are absolutely colorless, plainly showing lack of fresh air." Only in three hotels did the investigator report that the sleeping accommodations were good. In fourteen they were only fair, while in all of the others the girls complained of the crowded small rooms, of the poor ventilation and of the lack of bare necessities. In sixteen hotels from four to six girls slept in a small room originally designed for one bed. In one of these rooms the only furniture except the beds was a soap box. There was not even room for a chair. In most hotels two girls are made to sleep in the same bed. One girl may possess superior habits of cleanliness, yet no attention is paid to the protests she may make, nor to her demands for privacy and decency. Out of fifty hotels investigated, only in three did the women employees express satisfaction with the treatment received at the hands of the managers. In all the other places where the investigator interviewed the girls their reproaches and complaints were heartrending. In many instances the women were forced to work longer than the Ten-Hour Law permits. This was especially true in the hotels where the employees were foreigners. They themselves did not know of the Illinois Ten-Hour Law and they were warned not to speak to anyone about their work under penalty of dismissal. They were therefore afraid to tell the truth to the investigator. They could only murmur to her that they worked very long hours. Many of the forewomen admitted that some of their employees often worked overtime without extra pay.

Almost without exception the girls interviewed in the various hotels complained of the excessive hard work and the constant fatigue. Many of them stated that they were "so tired after the day's work that they did not care where they slept if they could only secure a bed on which to throw themselves." Others confessed to being so tired that they "did not take the trouble to undress."

The physical hardships endured by these girls are nothing compared to the moral dangers to which they are exposed. The girls who go to work in the hotels are for the most part decent and honest. They know that they will have to work hard and that their wages will be rather low, but they take the positions because they wish to earn an honest living. They are generally ignorant of the dangers in the hotels and yet, according to the testimony gathered by the investigator from housekeepers, very few of these originally honest girls come safely through the dangers to which they are constantly exposed.

The method employed by the investigator when visiting a hotel was to say to the housekeeper that she wanted to find a position for a young girl in whom she was interested, and almost without exception the housekeeper would say, "I would not advise you to put a young girl in a hotel. There are too many temptations and the girls are not able to resist them." Following are some of the remarks made by the housekeepers: "Unless a girl pays no attention to the remarks of the traveling men she will certainly go wrong." "I know of no occupation a girl can follow where she has the temptations which surround her in a hotel." "The temptations in a hotel are more than one can imagine. I do not like to see a girl led into temptation as she would be in a hotel." One elderly woman who had been a housekeeper for many years advised the investigator "not to get a position for a young girl any place where she could not stay home at night." "The majority of girls who work in hotels go wrong sooner or later," said one housekeeper. Another said, "Now, take it from me and don't send any young girl to work in a hotel in this neighborhood." "If only some of the women who write for the magazines knew half of the awful temptations which surround girls in hotels they would have something real to write about."

The majority of the managers of the hotels wink at the conduct of their guests and even connive at it. One housekeeper said that she knew for a positive fact that some of the chambermaids had been led into immorality by guests of the hotel.

Another said, "When off duty a girl could come and go as she pleased. No one took any interest in her—no one cared whether or not she was immoral." Another said, "No attention is ever paid to any complaint in regard to the immorality of the employees." One chambermaid said, in answer to a question put by the investigator, that the reason she had not complained to the manager of an outrageous insult she had received from one of the guests was "because I have two little children to support, and if we don't like the insults we get they'll tell us to clear out." In the majority of the hotels there seems to be almost a conspiracy to tempt the girl from the right path. In the first place, almost everything in her environment is bad. One housekeeper said that she "knew of many girls who met bad people in the hotel." Another said, "If the chambermaids are at all attractive they receive all kinds of invitations from guests."

"The kitchen girls come in contact with the waiters who do their utmost to spoil them." "Unless a girl makes up her mind to refuse every invitation she will almost surely go wrong." In many of the hotels there seems to be almost a premium put upon immorality. Not only is there no inducement to remain moral, but indeed rather the contrary. After a hard day's work, when a girl's muscles are fatigued and her nerves tense, she needs relaxation and rest to build her up for the next day's work. There is no opportunity for wholesome recreation or even rest.

Some of the girls complain and protest against this injustice. Said one chambermaid, "If a girl is straight there is nothing for her but bitter drudgery and no pleasure at all." "If a girl is good and refuses to go out there is absolutely nothing for her to do." "There is nothing for a girl in a hotel but work and sleep."

In some of the hotels the regulations almost drive the girl to an immoral life. In many hotels the employees come and go through a separate exit and many of these exits lead to dark alleys. Suspicious characters loiter in these places and the girl who might like to go somewhere in the evening is afraid to go out alone. She is obliged to seek the protection of an escort and oftentimes this escort is a man who has been persecuting her with his attentions. In many hotels the manager makes no attempt to prosecute the male employee who is responsible for the ruin of the girl employee. One decent girl in a hotel was found to be pregnant. The physician so advised the housekeeper and when the girl was told what was the matter she went to a physician and had an operation performed. She died at the Cook County Hospital in great agony. The manager of the hotel knew perfectly well the man who was responsible for this tragedy, but no action was taken. Another Polish girl, only fifteen years old, became pregnant. She was sent to the House of the Good Shepherd and there her child was born. The bellboy, only sixteen-years old, who was responsible for the affair, was allowed to disappear and no trace of him could be found. Many of these girls are perfectly innocent when they enter a hotel and the shortness of the period between the beginning of their service and the time of their downfall shows the terrible lack of moral standards in these places.

The great grievance of the majority of the girls is the excessively hard work. Not only the scrub-women, the kitchen girls and the laundry workers are worked to the limit of their endurance, but in many cases even the chambermaids are overtaxed as they often take care of thirty rooms. In one hotel the forewoman of the laundry admitted that the force was not nearly large enough for a hotel of that size and that the girls were therefore overworked. The bitter cry of all the workers is, "I am tired out all the time." "My back gets so tired." "I am so tired from backache that I can't stand up straight." "By bedtime I can scarcely stand."

WAITRESSES IN RESTAURANTS

The life of a girl who takes a position as waitress in a restaurant is almost as hard as that of a girl who works in a hotel. An investigator from the Juvenile Protective Association visited seventy-two restaurants in Chicago and interviewed girls in each of these places with a view of finding out the number of hours they worked, the wages paid them, the treatment accorded them by employers and customers, and the temptation by which they were surrounded.

The majority of the girls who become waitresses have had about the same amount of schooling as the average working woman. They usually live in furnished rooms, as they get their meals in the restaurants where they are employed. They go into the work for the following reasons: It does not require any skill; they get their meals away from home; the work has a certain amount of excitement and brings them in contact with a large number of people. The following are some of the replies to the question: "Why did you become a waitress?"

"Didn't know anything but waiting on table."

"The only thing I could do and be sure of three meals a day in addition to my wages."

"Only thing I could get."

"The only nice thing about work of this kind is that I get all kinds of invitations to go out and that helps some."

There is much complaint that the work is very hard and that the girls can only stand it for a few years.

The carrying of heavy trays and constant standing and walking causes ill health and trouble with the feet. Only comparatively few of the restaurants employing women as waitresses serve liquor to patrons. The waitresses who work in restaurants where liquor is sold are regarded as low-class by the other waitresses, and the excuse given by the former is that they receive larger tips where liquor is sold. The waitress does not require an education—not even as much training as a girl employed in domestic service, who must at least know the regular routine of housework and cooking. The manager often regards a pretty girl in the light of an attraction for his restaurant. In one place the pretty girls were put downstairs, where the men were served, and the homely girls were put upstairs, in the room reserved for women customers.

Many of the girls come from homes where they have had no training; others have left homes because they could not "get on" with their families; others because they lived in the country and wanted to come to the city where they felt there would be more recreation. Many of the girls, coming to know their own limitations and having no hope for a bright future, realize that they can expect but little in the way of wages and are therefore bent on having as good a time as possible while their youth and attractiveness last. When many girls, as the investigator discovered, reach this point of view it is no wonder that so many of them yield readily to temptation.

Owing to the recent decision of the United States Supreme Court affirming the Illinois ten-hour law for women, the restaurants are compelled by law not to work their women employees longer than ten hours a day. The waitresses are divided into steady workers—that is, those who work all day and are called "three-meal" girls, and those who work for part of the day and are called "one" or "two-meal" girls. Out of the 72 restaurants investigated it was found that 12 disregarded the ten-hours law. One worked its women employees 13 hours, five worked them 12 hours, two worked them 11 hours and four worked them 10 and a half hours. Thirty-four restaurants where steady workers were employed obeyed the ten-hour law. Twenty-seven of these gave their employees three hours off every afternoon, usually from 2 to 5 o'clock. The usual working hours are from 7 a. m. to 2 p. m. and from 5 p. m. to 8 p. m. The waitresses are therefore away from their homes from about 6 in the morning until 9 in the evening, allowing an hour to go to and from their work. It may readily be seen, therefore, what a very long and fatiguing day they have and how little opportunity it gives them for recreation or for the care of their person or clothes.

The greatest number of hours worked by these "full-time" waitresses was found to be 13, the lowest 6. In 16 restaurants they were obliged to work on Sundays. In one place they worked every other Sunday and in another half a day on Sunday. Of the 72 restaurants investigated 28 employed "part time" workers, or "one meal" girls. Three restaurants employed girls five hours a day. In four the girls worked four and a half hours a day.

Fifteen demanded five hours' work.

Six took three and a half hours of the waitresses' time. The longest period worked by these "part time" workers was five hours and the shortest three and a half hours.

The most noticeable fact in connection with the living conditions of these girls is the large number without homes. A large proportion of the waitresses who do live at home are engaged as "one-meal" girls. In many cases they are married women and when their children are at school and their husbands away at work they use the time to earn some money for themselves.

Many of the managers say that their waitresses belong to this class of women. One mother who was working as a "rush hours" waitress was in the habit of leaving her baby at home on a folded quilt in the bathtub.

In regard to wages it was found that out of the 72 restaurants the steady workers were paid as follows:

1 restaurant paid its girls $5.00 per week.

23 restaurants paid their girls $6.00 per week.

1 restaurant paid its girls $6.50 per week.

36 restaurants paid their girls $7.00 per week.

8 restaurants paid their girls $8.00 per week.

1 restaurant paid its girls $8.50 per week.

2 restaurants paid their girls $9.00 per week.

Of the wages paid to "part-time" workers it was found that 6 restaurants paid their girls $3.00 per week.

4 restaurants paid their girls $3.75 per week.

10 restaurants paid their girls $3.90 per week.

6 restaurants paid their girls $4.00 per week.

2 restaurants paid their girls $5.00 per week.

In most of these places there are few or no tips.

Ninety percent of the waitresses when asked about their work complained about one thing or another. The chief complaint was bad health brought about from being on their feet too long. Then came complaints of bad treatment by the public and following are some of the remarks: "People think they can say almost anything to a waitress." "Take any life but that of a waitress; they certainly get some hard knocks." "There is more to contend with in the life of a waitress than hard work." The other ten percent who did not complain said that the managers treated them decently, or that they belonged to the Union, or that the hours of work were not longer than six or eight hours. The ideas of the better class of waitresses may be learned from their remarks to the investigator. One girl said, "If I took all the men said to me the way they meant it I wouldn't be here long." Another said she would rather not take the tips than have to listen to the remarks of the young men who gave them.

Waitresses in a restaurant are apt to become "bold" in a short time, as can be seen by the remarks of the girls who evidently supplement their wages with the help of what they call their "gentleman friend," such as the following: "If I did not have a man I couldn't get along on my wages." "Some of the girls bat around and make nice money in other ways. I don't blame them, for they have to live." The experiences told the investigator are even more illuminating. One girl said, "A man who came to my restaurant asked me if I would not prefer to go to another position, where I would have more time and could wear pretty clothes." Another one said, "If I accepted all the invitations I get I wouldn't have time to sleep or eat." Some of the girls never come back for the money that is owing them after accepting one of the invitations. The investigator saw two young fellows who were served by a pretty girl trying to flirt with her. Before they left one of the men handed the girl a bill and said something. She shook her head and her face turned scarlet and the investigator heard the man say, "Oh, well, if you feel that way about it." Another said that a well-to-do businessman gave her to understand that if she wanted a good time he would see to it that she had it. In another place the investigator saw a man put his arm around a young waitress in a suggestive manner. She looked appealingly at the manager, but no protest was made.

Among the "part-time" workers are many who do something else besides serving as waitresses. Some study in the evening, either music, stenography, or telephone operating. A few fill two positions as waitresses. The arrangement is remnant of the time when steady waitresses were expected to work twelve and fourteen hours a day. By working in one place for dinner and another for luncheon they are able to obtain a few hours in between these two meals for themselves. They make more money working in two different places. For, instance, one manager would pay $3.90 a week for the luncheon hour and the same for the supper hour, while a girl working in one place for both these meals would receive only $6.00. Then, again, working at two places in one day breaks the monotony of the long day's work. Where the waitress is working at something else, as when she is practicing stenography in the evening, she is away from home the entire day and evening. Those girls who are not married and do not live at home, who work for only part of the day, have a hard time. One girl when asked how she managed to live said, "I live on $3.90? Well, I don't; and I'm not going to kill myself standing on my feet ten hours a day even to earn more."

TIPS SHOULD BE ABOLISHED

The giving of tips should be abolished because of their pernicious effect. A young girl who under any other circumstances would not dream of accepting money from a man will accept it in the guise of a tip. In the hands of a vicious man this tip establishes between him and the girl a relation of subservience and patronage which may easily be made the beginning of improper attentions. The most conscientious girl, dependent upon tips to eke out her slender wage, finds it difficult to determine just where the line of propriety is crossed. This, in addition to the other dangers surrounding the girl employed in hotels and restaurants they encounter that lack of respect which curiously attaches itself to one who accepts a gratuity.

The entire investigation revealed once more the hideous risk of the excessively fatigued and overworked girl who is able to obtain the rest and comfort she craves only through illicit channels.

All such testimony reveals the dangers in which many young girls are placed. The same kind-hearted people who would quickly gather in great concern around the victim of a street accident, carelessly eat food placed before them by a frail girl almost fainting with fatigue, or heedlessly walk through a hotel corridor lately scrubbed by a Polish woman who has spent ten hours upon her hands and knees. They do not in the least realize that the loss of vitality and life itself in the latter, is quite as harrowing as in the former. Only when the public learns to know the effects of protracted labor upon women engaged in hotels and restaurants, will adequate measures be taken for their relief. This pamphlet is issued in the hope that its publication may hasten the day when help will come for these overburdened girls.

WHAT'S TO BE DONE?

At present our conditions are deplorable. It is only possible to remedy them ourselves. How shall we go about it?

Pleading with our bosses won't do it. Electing politicians to act for us is a waste of time and energy. To expect other workers who are organized to help us, while not attempting to help ourselves, is futile and cowardly. *We must do the thing ourselves*. We must follow the lines of *Agitation, Organization,* and *Education*.

We must arouse the workers to the necessity of action. This will lead to organization. Then we must teach the workers methods of using their organization.

Just any kind of an organization won't do. We must have a fighting, revolutionary, industrial union. A modern weapon, for a modern age. We want a union that will promote the solidarity of the workers, not divide them. A union that will take into its fold every man, woman, and child, regardless of age, color or creed, that works in this industry. It is much more important that the dishwashers, busboys and pantry-girls quit work when the waiters and cooks go out on strike than it is for the waiters and cooks to have the sympathy of union scabs who are delivering supplies to the house.

Hotel and restaurant workers have been the victims of craft union inefficiency and blunders so many times that many of them have become hostile to the union idea. In nearly every strike in this industry, engineered by craft unionists, the workers have lost. Craft union waiters have gone out on strike and union cooks working under a contract have helped defeat them, and vice-versa. Sometimes the cooks and waiters have struck together only to have their places filled by the busboys, dishwashers, pantry-girls etc., who were considered too unimportant to organize. Often these unorganized workers have quit work to help the craft union workers win but never have the craft unionists sought to help them. Craft union waiters and cooks usually treat the busboys, dishwashers, porters and pantry help with contempt, thereby making an excuse for these workers to scab in time of strike. They want to get even. I repeat here that this is one industry where craft unions have not and can not function.

The industrial union form of organization, with a revolutionary program, with a splendid fighting spirit and modern tactics, is our only hope. This form of union encourages solidarity, it breathes the spirit of *An Injury to One is an Injury to All*. And this is the motto of the Industrial Workers of the World. To give you an idea of what the IWW is, I shall quote from some of its literature.

No terms made with an employer are final. All peace so long as the wage system lasts is but an armed truce. The Industrial Workers realize that the day of successful long strikes is past. Under all ordinary circumstances a strike that is not won in four to six weeks cannot be won by remaining out longer.

The organization does not allow any part to enter into time contracts with the employers. The Industrial Workers of the World maintains that nothing will be conceded by the employers except that which we have the power to take and hold by the strength of our organization. Therefore we seek no agreements with the employers.

In the IWW low dues are always the rule, low initiation fees likewise. Every inducement to join that can be offered to the workers is offered by the IWW

Another feature of the IWW is the universal transfer of cards. A member of the IWW can transfer from one industrial union to another of the same or different industry, without cost. One union, one card. Once a union man, always a union man.

HOW TO ORGANIZE

The Hotel, Restaurant Workers, and Domestics Industrial Union has headquarters in Chicago, and branches in many cities throughout the country. If you are employed in a hotel, restaurant, cafeteria, club or private home, and you are not a member of this organization, it is your duty to become one at once. If there is not a delegate of this union in the place where you work, address headquarters for information on how to organize.

This general information may help you. First: become a member yourself. Second: read our literature, get acquainted with the principles of industrial unionism, subscribe for at least one of our papers, talk about what you have learned to the workers around you, soon you will have them interested. Third: you should become a delegate of this union; we will furnish you with credentials. You will then have very little trouble in building up the organization in the place where you work. Through these methods we are building up a splendid organization; our membership is growing rapidly. We have no high salaried organizers; we do not furnish deluxe club rooms.

TRUTH, AN EFFICIENT WEAPON

Little bits of chicken
That most of us forget,
Gathered by the careful cook
Make a swell croquette.

Don't you think the boss would raise our wages before he would let us tell his guests just how the food that they eat was prepared?

Suppose we asked for shorter hours and the boss refused, and we had a little circular printed explaining the mysteries of the kitchen. Say that we told that the stock for all the fine soups and sauces comes from a large boiler filled with chicken heads, feet and sometimes entrails. That the ends of unwashed vegetables, pieces of putrid meat and rotten tomatoes are always thrown in the stock boiler. Suppose that we tell the truth and say that the kitchen is overrun with rats and that they nibble continually at the food.

What if we tell that oysters are dipped in water that is often filthy and slimy, to freshen them; that chickens and fish that smell rotten are covered with lemon juice to kill the smell, that eggs that should be buried are used in the bake shop, that the butter that comes back from the dining room is used again and that the napkins that have been used, possibly by a consumptive, are used to wipe the dishes with, and a hundred other things that we know and they don't? What do you think would happen to the boss? Don't you think that he would raise your wages rather than lose his trade?

THE SERVANT PROBLEM

We hear a lot of talk nowadays about the "Servant Problem."

The masters are having trouble with the workers they dub "the Serving Class." They can't understand why servants should complain about their conditions. What matters it, if servants are abused and insulted, if they work twelve to fourteen hours a day, for damn near nothing? The masters are like the Queen who said, "if the people have not bread, let them eat cake"; they do not understand the situation. They cannot grasp the simple fact, that servants really belong to the species of man, that they have the five senses, a brain and a heart, and that they love and hate, like any other human being.

I shall waste no time in trying to educate our ignorant masters. My argument is with my fellow workers; we have the power to do away with masters, if we use it intelligently. Therefore I will address my reasoning to the workers, in the hope that it will enable them to solve the "Servant Problem" to their own satisfaction.

The causes of discontent among servants are manifold and universal. Take, for instance, the household or domestic servant; the condition of these workers is deplorable. Taken as a whole, the wages are lowest and the hours are longest of any workers.

Their duties are undoubtedly degrading. Servility and obedience are essential qualities in servants.

Their labors consist in doing the things their masters consider too degrading to do for themselves. They scrub, sweep and clean their homes. They prepare, cook and serve their meals. They are both nurse and plaything of the master's children. They are gardener and coachman, and groom to dogs and horses. The servants wash and iron the master's clothes, shine their shoes, clean cuspidors, polish silver, exercise the dog, and humiliate themselves in a multitude of ways. All this is done with the meekest of servility. They are truly menials, or I should say they have been, for fortunately servants are beginning to feel the ignominy of their position.

The master's household is becoming more discordant daily, and the reasons are apparent to the thoughtful observer.

The children of rich families usually treat the servants of the house with domineering words, names of contempt, and imperious carriage; as if they were of another race or species beneath them. The example of the masters, the advantage of fortune, and vanity inspires this haughtiness.

William Penn, in "Fruits of Solitude" says,

> The least thing out of joint or omitted, makes us uneasy and we are ready to think ourselves ill served, about that which is of no real service at all. Let not thy children domineer over thy servants… When the poor Indians hear us call any of our family by the name of servants, they cry out, 'What call thy brethren servants! We call our dogs, servants, but never men.'

But the Indians had not been cursed with a religion that teaches that servility and meekness are virtues in those who toil.

And if the Indians were here today, they would hear the rich call their servants names that would make an Indian's dog blush with shame.

Emerson saw the evil results of menial labor, when he wrote:

> We allow ourselves to be served by them. We live apart from them, and meet them without salute in the streets. We do not greet their talents nor in the assembly of the people vote for what is dear to them. Thus we enact the part of the selfish noble and king from the foundation of the world. See, this tree always bears one fruit. In every household the peace of a pair is poisoned by the malice, slyness, indolence, and alienation of domestics. Let any two matrons meet, and observe how soon their conversation turns to the troubles from their 'Help,' as our phrase is.

To say that the rich are enacting the part of the selfish noble and king is putting it mildly. For these plutocrats are "but a rotten imitation of the middle ages." They treat us like chattel slaves. They compel us to work long hours, feed us poorly, and inflict personal abuse upon us.

These soulless parasites call us the "Serving Class." They make scrub women of our mothers, and take our sisters and daughters into their mansions as servants, to do the bidding of their pampered and sybaritic daughters, and to be subject to the lustful advances of their degenerate, bestial, brainstormed scions. With the whip of want and hunger they beat our sons and brothers into submission and servility, to become their lackeys, to serve as valet, butler, etc. And if we should complain they accuse us of ingratitude and viciousness, they stigmatize us as ungrateful, discontented, disobedient servants.

Why should servants be grateful for the crumbs that fall from the rich man's table? They should be seated at the board and they know it. As for being discontented, a man who would not be discontented with such surroundings and such a low mode of life would be a perfect brute. It is through disobedience that progress has been made, through disobedience and rebellion. Disobedience in the eyes of any one who has read history is man's original virtue.

A servant ungrateful, discontented and rebellious, is probably a real personality and has much in him. The obedient and servile servant cannot be admired—even the master, who may be glad to have such a servant, cannot possibly respect him.

I have inferred that girl servants in the homes of the rich are used for immoral purposes. It is a fact that some rich parents select the healthiest and prettiest maids as an inducement to keep their sons at home and out of the rowdy houses of the district. Recently, Miss M. L. Carpenter of Chicago made the startling statement that 75 percent of the women of the tenderloin of the cities in the United States are recruited from domestic service. Miss Carpenter, who spent nine months in the kitchens of Chicago for the purpose of making a study of the situation, declared that the women of America were dormant to a condition which has existed for years, and upon which disorderly houses throughout the land flourish. Girls who come from the country and get employment in private homes are unsafe. They are menaced by the heads of families, or older sons, and this, together with long hours, late dinners in the houses where they are in service, and often orgies, lead to their ultimate degradation.

Such is the morality of the rich. Volumes might be written on this one phase of servant life. This crime against the sisters of the workers is being exploited by the modern dramatist. I refer you to John Galsworthy's significant play "The Eldest Son" and Henrik Ibsen's masterpiece "Ghosts." Also Leo Tolstoi's powerful novel *Resurrection.*

The maid in the homes of the rich who has not been approached or insulted is indeed the exception. It is a waste of time and energy to try and patch up the differences between masters and servants; they have no common ground. No self-respecting human being will ever be satisfied to remain the menial servant of another. We must organize to make better the condition of servants now, and, finally, do away with menial labor.

WHERE DO YOU BELONG?

Do you belong in somebody's kitchen, attic, or basement, doing their dirty work, attending to their most intimate personal needs, hiring out for all the time you are awake into the services of others who treat you as an inferior being?

Do you belong there? Are you satisfied with your lot? Are you content to be a slave?

Or do you wish to have shorter hours, higher wages, and respectful treatment from your employers?

If so, do you belong to the Domestic Workers Industrial Union (IWW), an organization of domestic slaves who have broken away from monotonous drudgery of their existence, who have rebelled at outrages imposed on them, and have banded together in a determined effort to better their conditions.

They realize that their only hope lies in arousing the workers to a knowledge of their own power, and that their only strength lies in organization. They invite you to join them, knowing that your wrongs are their wrongs, and that an injury to one is an injury to all. Don't hold back and allow them to fight your battles. Don't sit idly by while they struggle against the enemy, which is your enemy, and then step forward in the end and reap the benefits you don't deserve.

Endorse them, support them, join them. That is where your interest lies. Have you served others so long you have forgotten you have interests of your own? Join the IWW's Domestic Workers Industrial Union. They need you and you need them. *That is where you belong.*

It includes housemaids, cooks, second girls, nursemaids, laundresses, seamstresses, and all workers engaged by the hour, day or month in private families.

IWW, Chicago, 1918

From Chumley's 1918 *Hotel and Restaurant Workers* pamphlet
(cartoon by "Dust" Wallin)

JIM SEYMOUR

The Dishwasher

Alone in the kitchen, in grease-laden steam,
I pause for a moment—a moment to dream,
For even a dishwasher thinks of a day
Wherein there'll be leisure for rest and for play.
And now that I pause, o'er the transom there floats,
A strain of the Traumerie's soul-stirring notes.
Engulfed in a blending of sorrow and glee,
I wonder that music can reach even me.

For now I am thinking; my brain has been stirred,
The voice of a master the lowly has heard.
The heart-breaking sobs of the sad violin,
Arouses the thoughts of the sweet "might-have-been."
Had men been born equal, the use of their brain
Would shield them from poverty, free them from pain,
Nor would I have sunk in the black social mire
Because of poor judgment in choosing a sire.

But now I am only a slave of the mill
That piles and remodels me just as it will;
That makes me a dullard in brain-burning heat;
That looks at rich viands not daring to eat;
That works with his red, blistered hands ever stuck
Down deep in the foul indescribable muck
Where dishes are plunged seventeen at a time,
And washed!—in a tubful of sickening slime.

But on with your clatter! no more must I shirk,
The world is to me but a nightmare of work.
For me not the music, the laughter and song,
No toiler is welcome amid the gay throng.
For me not the smiles of the ladies who dine
No sweet clinging kisses begotten of wine.
For me but the venting of low sweated groans
That twelve hours a night have instilled in my bones.

The music has ceased but the havoc it wrought
Within this poor brain it awakened to thought,
Shall cease not at all, but continue to spread
Till all of my fellows are thinking or dead.
The havoc it wrought, 'Twill be havoc to those
Whose joys would be nil were it not for my woes.
Keep on with your gorging, your laughter and jest,
But never forget that the last laugh is best.

You leeches that live on the fat of the land,
You overfed parasites, look at my hands.
You laugh at them now they are blistered and coarse;
But such are the hands quite familiar with force;
And such are the hands that have furnished you drink
The hands of the slaves who are learning to think,
And hands that have fed you can crush you as well
And cast your damned carcasses clear into hell!

Go on with your scoffing begotten of gold;
As now are your hearts, will your bodies be cold.
Go on with your scorning, you creators of hate
Eat well while the dishwasher spits on your plate.
And while at your feast let the orchestra play
The life-giving strains of the dear Marseillaise,
Let the red revolution be placed on the throne
Till those who produce have come to their own.

But scorn me tonight, in the morn you shall learn
That those whom you loathe can despise you in turn.
The dishwasher vows that his fellows shall know
That only their ignorance keeps them below.
Your music was potent, your music hath charms,
It hardened the muscles that strengthen my arms;
It painted a vision of freedom, of life—
Tomorrow we strive for the ending of strife!

First published in the *Industrial Worker*, May 1, 1913; the text here incorporates later changes made by the author.

JIM SEYMOUR

R-R-R-Raw Food!

What do you say we go out for a lunch? Yes, I know it's too hot to eat, but if Billy Sunday's dope is straight it'll be even hotter for us if we don't eat. Now don't start that everlasting pow-wow about which restaurant or which other one. I reckon I know that catalog of grease-joints about as well as you do. There's the Royal Gorge, the Greasy Spoon, Stuffer's, the Microscopic Portion, the Chew Shoe Noodeleria, and so forth *ad indigestum.*

Huh? Say that again. A raw food eating-house, eh? Langdon Smith's *Evolution* must have gotten on your nerves. Do you really believe that there has been so sudden and so general a reversion to type that someone finds it profitable to cater to the needs of the disveneered? A beautiful picture this genial California sun is burning into your brain: savages tearing the bleeding flesh of the newly-killed prey; loud-smelling entrails scattered over mosaic tiling; protruding chops dripping with fresh warm blood; hairy claws clutching great chunks of red, quivering—ugh! cut it out!

Well, why didn't you *say* so? If that's the case I don't mind trying it. Why, it's right across the street—that sign reading "Eat Your Way to Health." Reminds me of the time I was hog-tied and a little bird said, "Gnaw your way to freedom."

Draw a long breath. Now—we're in! And as we sometimes are signpainters and are governed by economic determinism—yes, yes, we talk shop—the first thing we see is a sign bearing the startling announcement, "We feed our hogs scientifically." But don't be offended too soon. They are not calling us names; they are merely advising us to curb our appetites and eat like hogs. See? —the rest of the sign reads, "How many of us eat scientifically?"

There is another unusual sign that reads, "Do you care to read while eating? You are welcome to take any of our books from the literature table and read during your meal." On the table are books, both cheap and expensive. Help yourself. They are all for sale, we learn, but you will never know it unless you are interested enough to inquire, for here the commercial spirit is strangely lacking.

In the cheeks of the woman behind the counter we notice a rosy bloom that is the real thing. Don't get poetical now. We're talking about grub and this is no IWW convention.

Grab your tray, old-timer; we savvy that much anyhow. We ask about this first dish and the lady explains that it is called pemmican, is made of crushed nuts and grains, and is served with this banana sauce. We'll try pemmican. And from the salads and salads we select a couple and a portion of raw carrots. Moving down the line we boldly appropriate a slab of raw pie and then proceed somewhat less boldly toward the cash register.

Beside the register are the drinks and behind it a young man who looks good to us—good enough to call Phil right off the bat. Phil doesn't resent it a bit; in fact, it seems to go straight to the warm spot in his democratic core. We ask him if these drinks aren't pretty raw and he assures us that they are. We fail to find any raw booze among them, but there are grape and orange juices, goat's milk and cow's milk. Noticing our hesitation, Phil gives us the quick once-over and recommends not the most expensive drink, but the cheapest. Peculiar fellow, this Phil. He knows we will accept his diagnosis at 'most any old price, but he seems to prefer principles to a few pennies of profit.

We pay thirty-nine cents for our feed and retire to a nice clean table. We are much surprised to discover that the food is remarkably palatable, especially the carrots. We can't figure out how the carrots are prepared, but they are great stuff. And we are more surprised to learn that we have ordered more food than we can eat. It has a kick that is amazing and that teaches us the futility of attempting to gobble everything we see simply because we happen to have the price. How do stockmen feed hogs scientifically? Good food and less of it.

Really, I don't believe we'll be able to walk for fifteen minutes or so, so we'll look over the literature. Look here—these people are not merely food-peddlers; they are dreamers, and their dream is scientific. We haven't time right now to read it all, but it seems they dream of a world of beauty, of love, and of happiness; of a world of intelligence and the sense of justice that generally accompanies intelligence. They dream of a world free from all diseases, including ignorance and yellow journalism. And they dream of a world where murder is murder, regardless of the number of feet possessed by the murdered creature. On the whole, these people are quite different from the gentlemen of the beef trust who spend millions of dollars in advertisements announcing that they are in business for their health.

Well, we'll be going. And listen, people: Yours is a fine and noble work and we're with you strong, but don't forget that when we are out of a job and haven't the price of a plate of raw food our goose is cooked. That little kink in the problem must also be straightened. We're with you, people; are *you* with us? If so, let's plug together for the economic permission to eat good food, raw and unseasoned, and to become the salt of the Earth.

The New Justice, No. 13, Los Angeles, August 15, 1919

"Two eggs, three-minute boiled. Hurry! Only got one minute to catch my train."
(cartoon by Art Young)

HUMANIST MEETING

CHICAGO CHAPTER, (Number One)
THE AMERICAN HUMANIST ASSOCIATION

YOU WILL WANT TO BE THERE

with **JACK SHERIDAN** at

"Breakfast With Destiny"

FRIDAY, MAY 20, 1960
TOFFANETTI'S - Private Dining Room
72 West Randolph, Chicago, Illinois

Publicity for a Lecture based on
Jack Sheridan's 1959 *Industrial Worker* series,
"Breakfast With Destiny"

JACK SHERIDAN

Breakfast with Destiny

PART I

All history that is true history was once life, so history should prove itself again in life. Let us consider history as it affects the breakfast table—our own by preference.

When we get out of bed we pay compliments to Egypt in two respects. In the first place, the idea of a bed was first conceived by a Nile craftsman, and secondly "time" was worked out by an Egyptian mathematician. Sheets being made of cotton can be dated at 3,000 years before Christ by a fragment of cloth found in the ruined city of Mojendo-Daro in the Indus Valley. Ram's head seals and a lamb stew, found in an earthen covered pot in Telasmar, Asia Minor, imply a date for wool at least 4,000 years B.C. and add a long tradition to your blanket. And your pajamas or nightgown, you may reflect, were sewn by a needle—an invention which belongs to the last Ice Age of Europe, or over 40,000 years ago.

No doubt you are going to have orange juice for breakfast. Our word "orange" is derived from the Persian *auransa.* It is suspected that we learned about oranges in one of those looting expeditions of our ancestors during the Crusades of the eleventh century, but the word is still more ancient. *Auransa* is Sanskrit, the mother of all languages of Europe from the ancient Greeks to the jargon of the most beat of beatniks.

That orange juice you drink out of a glass. Beads of glass have been found in Egypt dated by some learned men at 3500 B.C. Molded glass is rather less ancient. Workingstiffs were blowing glass in Syria about the time that Paul was preaching to the Corinthians.

Septimus Severus, Emperor of the Romans and of Libyan birth, visiting his loyal city of Alexandria, saw with great satisfaction the prosperous glass industry of the city. Like all rulers who like security he was anxious to promote commerce, so he put a stiff tax on glass and with the proceeds built himself and his relatives some very fine palaces. By this small act he made glass very valuable and a great luxury which all the people wished to possess. Governments do similar things with postage stamps today, from which we learn that the science of government is less difficult than we generally believe.

While we are on the subject it will not do any harm to say that most government is unnecessary labor—if officials would only leave the people alone, they would manage and govern their affairs much more efficiently.

As we're seated at breakfast and admiring the ingenuity of Severus, we are sitting on a chair and this is somewhat indirectly paying Egypt another compliment. At the moment I have in mind a particular chair which is known as "American Empire" and was made in 1820, copied from a French Empire chair made in 1810. The chair maker got his idea from bronze chairs made in Egypt 4,000 years ago and looted from the Pyramids by Napoleon in the latter part of the eighteenth century.

Somehow or other oatmeal has been associated with Scotsmen but oats are not Scottish. Vavilof, an investigator of such matters, has placed the origin of oats in the Chinese highlands. They were brought to Scotland in the late Bronze or early Iron Age. Now the habits of the Scots in regard to other people's sheep made their own highlands attractive residences, and oats grow on mountains better than other grains. China is also the home from which the dish that contains the oatmeal came. This matter of chinaware is a little involved. China received from Arabia a substance related to glass, known as "glaze," which Arabia originally got from Egypt.

In the Near East this resulted in the famous Murrine ware which delighted the fashionable Mediterranean world, which led to a poem about it by Pro Pen Shus. The story which the poem relates is that a lady who did her day's work at night offered a very desirable maiden the wealth of the Orient if she would be one of her hostesses in her houses of assignation; purple robes, silk dresses from the Islands of Cos, and Murrine goblets baked in Parthian furnaces were the rewards of her compliance. Centuries later another poet, Joe Hill, was to write a song on this age-old theme of sex in the market place.

At first, China created substantial wheel-turned vases coated with Arabian glaze, but a few hundred years later produced porcelain. The Portuguese brought china or porcelain back to Europe in the sixteenth century and you can now buy it in any five-and-ten cent store, and no one would think of offering it to a lady for her favors.

If you have toast for breakfast, the hard wheat originally came from Abyssinia, the soft from Afghanistan. You owe your egg to a bird known to the Greeks as the Persian fowl, but in reality it was the jungle cock of India, which the Hindus domesticated before there were Greeks or Persians.

Coffee was once a wild bean in Abyssinia. In the fourteenth century it passed over into Arabia and was met with a theological blast almost as violent as that which in a century later King James met up with when he received the gracious lady nicotine. The civil governors of Arabia, anxious to support the men of religion, passed stern laws against the use of coffee, and collected baksheesh, or whatever was the synonym for graft in fourteenth-century Arabia, from those Arabs who just had to have their morning coffee.

The Dutch found coffee drinking so well established in Arabia that they decided to take the bean to Java, where a worm ate it, and ultimately to Brazil and Central America. During the depression and economic chastisement of the 1930s, the Brazilian economists conceived some truly inspiring ideas about this soothing and stimulating narcotic. They burned this once-Abyssinian berry under the boilers of Amazon steamers in order to let these steamers collect more coffee to burn under boilers in order to collect more coffee—this is a confused explanation, but so were the minds of the Brazilian economists. Statistically stated, it worked out something about this way. In 1929 the United States paid about 300 million dollars for 700,000 tons of coffee. In 1932 the United States paid 130 million dollars, about one-third as much money, for about 750,000 tons of coffee or 50,000 more tons of the same kind of berry, but not the same kind of money.

You, perhaps, take sugar in your coffee. Herodotus, who lived in 450 B.C., refers to sugar as "honey made without the aid of a bee." The Chinese called it "stone honey" since they received it from the Persians in hard brown lumps. In a trade guide written about the year 60, it is spoken of as honey from the reed saccharina which is the same as sugar that comes from sugar cane. The Arabs brought the sugar cane from southeastern Asia and Palestine and ultimately to the once fortunate islands of the ancients now known as the Canaries. The Arabs also imported Negro slaves to tend the cauldrons. It was here on the Canary Islands that the Portuguese in the fifteenth century found and approved of both—the slaves and the sugar-making.

Taking advantage of the Pope's mistakes in map-making, the Portuguese imported sugar cane, sugar-making and slaves to their new colony of Brazil in the sixteenth century. From Brazil sugar making spread to the French, Dutch and English islands, and sugar planters became the rich aristocracy of the seventeenth century.

The supplying of sugar plantations with Negro slaves from Africa became a most profitable trade in the seventeenth century. Land on these islands became too valuable for anything but the growing of sugar, so food for the slaves had to be imported. Yankee traders from New York and Pennsylvania fed these natives with Indian corn, salt fish, pork and beef and supplied them with staves to make casks, also horses and knock-down houses, and even small sailing vessels. In exchange these Yankee traders received tropical products such as cotton, molasses and rare woods. And, from the Spanish islands in particular, they received silver, bullion and coins.

These various forms of wealth, together with bills of exchange the islands had received for sugar shipments, were used by American traders to balance their merchandising accounts with England. The navigation laws ordered that all colonial goods should land in England and excise duties to be paid before shipment to foreign ports. Hence, the colonial trade with the islands and countries of Central and South America, according to English law, was illegal. The English statesmen called Americans engaged in this trade all sorts of unsavory names, such as smugglers, pirates, blockade runners and buccaneers. Many American shipowners and shipmasters were hanged on these or similar charges enforced by English law.

Now let us examine this in its concatenations just merely to bring out the salient features of the relationship of law to circumstances. First of all, the land that lay along the Atlantic seaboard in what is now the United States was taken and populated by English merchant adventurers. The fruits of their conquests they secured and bulwarked with the British Navy, but after these merchant adventurers had been established here for some time they came to regard it as home and, looking about for opportunities to trade, found them in the southerly seas of the Americas at least one thousand miles from the argus-eyed English officials. If this trade was carried on and no noise was made about it, the traders and the shipowners were relieved of paying taxes, duties, demurrage, and space assessments. That is, the American shipmasters dealing in the ports of the Spanish Main saved thousands of dollars that would, under law, flow into the Island of England. The English found this out and passed navigation acts covering this practice, making it illegal to trade in the southern part of the western world without first paying tribute to London.

To evade the law the American seamen became smugglers—also rich—and began publishing newspapers and books advocating independence, meaning independence of British lawmakers. After fifty years of propaganda and eight years of armed conflict, they set aside one day in the year which they call "Independence Day," so it comes about each Fourth of July we become very indignant about tyranny and go into raptures with considerable noise celebrating our freedom from the English.

Our American Revolution, around which so much sentiment has been engendered, and which our school books are devoted to and about which our natives go into rhapsody, is in reality a by-product of the sugar and slave trade.

Some Fourth of July when the American working man has nothing else to do he should look up the meaning of the word "independence" and how it came to be wed to politics. Then he should get down off the library shelves about two tons of history books and political writings dating back to 1620, and follow the concept, the meaning and application of political ideas to everyday concerns. With this accomplished he would become a competent Fourth of July orator, although his audience in their blindness would mob him.

PART II

In the first installment of this series, some of the items that appear on our breakfast table were traced back to their origins and among other things it was hinted that the American revolution was a by-product of the sugar and slave trade. Now to go on with our breakfast.

Historically speaking, "Independence" is only one of a hundred similar political concepts, but if our workingman will master the technique of this one, he will have the key to "the just price," "the divine right of kings," "the drive to the east," "realism and humanism," and a host of other political concepts that seem to perplex our attempts to understand the nature of the economic forces under which we live.

When Hitler got hold of one of these political concepts he became so enthusiastic about it that he overlooked all the material forces arrayed against him. It led him from obscurity and insignificance to notoriety and importance, and finally to his downfall and death.

Hitler's career, historically speaking, is commonplace. He failed like so many before him. Occasionally some succeed like Washington, Franklin and Adams. Those who succeed do so because they are able to judge the strength of the forces arrayed against them.

The Hindus, who have a happy faculty of expressing general ideas, place all these enthusiasms about these political concepts under the word *chorozon* meaning that man's imagination becomes so inflamed that he overlooks the strength of the opposition and *chorozon* tears him to pieces.

Political concepts such as Liberty, Equality, Fraternity, Brotherhood, Nationalism, and Free Enterprise have a practical, material base and the man who wanders too far from the base will find *chorozon* there with the ball to put him out.

Let's get back to our breakfast. Most of the sugar from the United States comes from *beta vulgaris* or sugar beets. Where do sugar beets grow best? In the west, in the vicinity of the Rocky Mountains, where water from the melting glaciers gives the required moisture. In 1873, during the great panic, the Mormon

Church borrowed $300,000 and built a sugar beet refinery and it is now one of the big factories in the sugar trade. Candolle, a Swiss botanist, said that sugar beets came from the Caspian sea about 400 B.C.

Well, we are about ready to read the news. We open the morning paper and it plunks us right down into the middle of modern times. Men backed by every device of science have gathered, collected and dispatched, edited and printed for us every horror, terror, and scandal from all over the world and brought it to our breakfast table for a few pennies. This is democracy, the free press and the "fourth estate," so they say. But paper is Chinese, from the second century, and movable cast metal type was invented and used in Korea a hundred years before Gutenberg or Caxton started their experiments with the printed word.

With humble satisfaction we light our after-breakfast cigarette. Cigarettes and tobacco are both American and if we were real downright patriots that's all we would have for breakfast, cancer scare or no cancer scare. All the rest is of far foreign origin. Other peoples of the world discovered, invented and first used all the other items that went into the making of our breakfast. Yet that is not the nub of the matter, and in case we have overlooked it no harm will be done if we revert to it. Our breakfast is the end result of *production*. Our breakfast is one of the daily incidents in our sustenance. It is very commonplace and happens so frequently that we all eat our breakfast with little or no philosophizing. In fact, most people do not associate philosophy with breakfast at all. But breakfast, with our other meals, including other matters that sustain us, are more important than all the philosophies that have ever been devised.

Somehow or other the average workingman, when he thinks of progress or civilization, imagines it originated with religion, philosophy, education or some similar mental discipline. He concludes, for instance, that the reason we are civilized is because we are educated and the reason we are educated is that we are the smartest people in the world. As a corollary, he goes one step further. He feels, when "we Americans" carry education to other parts of the world, that trouble and strife will be over.

For the average workingman, education is a cure-all, a sovereign remedy that can be applied to all social and political ills. Ever since the Soviets got a sputnik into space we have come to look upon education as some kind of a god who performs miracles. Education has become the fetish of modern man and we accept it with the same reverence and unreasoning devotion as our primitive forebears gave to their charms and amulets. It is no uncommon experience to hear propagandists of all political parties proclaim the proficiency of education. It is amazing how widespread this particular superstition is, and it is still more amazing the tenacity with which most workers cling to it.

Education has none of the prime virtues attributed to it. Properly speaking, all that education is, is a method of social control, a way of guiding efforts so that the upper or ruling class will derive benefits from collective effort. Even at that it is a poor stick and hopelessly inefficient.

Education is essentially a discipline, and as such, is organically negative. That is, it produces meager results at tremendous costs and effort. Steam locomotives are an analogous example. They require attention, burn tremendous amounts of fuel, eat up energy with an avaricious maw and return at the maximum, less than 20 percent as work performed. Education similarly, only on an elaborate and grander scale, works in the same manner, except its yield is something under 3 percent. Presuming that a worker had some knowledge of the law of parsimony he would be struck dumb with astonishment that so much effort would be put forth to obtain the mite of progress attained.

The writer of this piece recently observed the five hundred students of a small college assemble. He studied their actions, how they came to be assembled and their ultimate destiny. Here are a few of the items involved: Clothes and food for 500 students, space in the street for buses and automobiles, years of training for competent instructors and 500 times four years for each student. Make a rough calculation of it and one can readily see the energy put forth to train even so small a body as 500 students. What is the end result? One engineer, one chemist, 19 accountants, 75 stenographers and 400 salesmen who will sell goods for a master. Figured in social efficiency that is something less than 3 percent. So coming back to our breakfast with destiny, one can readily realize how much more important and decisive are products and their creation, socially speaking. Out of a breakfast we at least obtain some sustenance; something is returned to us that is really helpful to us, but our education is simply a device by which we give our lives to the end that the owners of property and industry grow richer.

PART III

Well, if you carefully read the second article in this series, you at least learned a new word, *chorozon*. You also learned that all political concepts, regardless of the phraseology they are dressed up in, have a practical, material base. The author also hinted at why politicians like Washington, Franklin and Adams succeeded, while other politicians, such as Hitler, failed. The second article also contained some very harsh remarks about our educational system.

Until the Portuguese navigators in the sixteenth century opened ocean trade with the Far East, the caravan routes across higher Asia were the earth's greatest culture roads. In order to get a clear picture of this ancient trade, we must bear in mind the fact that China already knew something about Europe through her trade with Java and Ceylon, where her merchants met the daring Moorish traders from Arabia. China imported gum storax from the land of Punt, rhinoceros horns, African ivory, the glaze for her first venture in porcelain and many other things.

The Chinese had heard of Spain and believed that the merino sheep were seven feet high. The Chinese knew of the Mediterranean and the Atlantic. Chinese merchants had knowledge of the great Portuguese ships, then trading on the western coast of Africa and which were later to circumnavigate the globe. The Chinese called Arabia "the land of the western sun from whence all good things come." China knew more about Europe and the west than Europe was to know about China for more than a thousand years, and she wanted to learn more.

When her generals and commercial explorers arrived overland at the Persian Gulf they wanted to sail on to Rome, but the Persians were businessmen with no idea of losing their profits as middle-men, so they told the credulous Chinese that the journey to Rome took two to three years and was very dangerous. As every good Chinese wanted to be buried within the border of the Celestial Empire a voyage of such danger cooled the desire for geographic knowledge. Actually such a journey took about three months and men had been taking it for two, maybe three thousand years.

The exchanges between China and the West were among the most fruitful of all cultural contacts and in these exchanges China was by no means the loser. In a remote period China had received from the West the chariot wheel and its variants, the potter's wheel and the spinning wheel. The horse saddle and harness were also among the West's gifts to China. Silk, rag paper, block printing, movable type and paper money were China's gifts to the West. China received glass and glaze from Arabia or Egypt and returned it as porcelain to the West at a later period.

The use of paper and movable type appear among the most characteristic features of Western culture. Yet the West owes them to the Far East. In the first century after Christ, a Chinese chamberlain, annoyed at the cost and inconvenience of bamboo on which to keep records and accounts of the Celestial Court, invented or accepted the invention of paper. He was the eunuch Say Lun, not unworthy of fame, and of him it is said:

"In ancient times writing was on bamboo or on pieces of silk which were called chits, but silk being expensive and bamboo heavy these two materials were not convenient for keeping records or accounts, so Say Lun thought of using tree bark, hemp, rags and fish nets. In the first year of Yuan, that is, 105 A.D., he made a report to the Emperor on the process of paper making and received high praise for his ability. From this time paper has been in use everywhere and is called the paper of Say Lun." It is further recorded of this fellow Say Lun that becoming involved in a court intrigue and wishing to avoid an appearance before the judges he went home, took a bath, combed his hair, put on his best robes and drank poison, which, of course, is typical of a Chinese who has the least suspicion against his name.

Professor Carter, who made a special study of paper, has given us a most significantly dated map of the distribution of paper. It starts in China in 105 A.D. and arrives in Turfan on the old trade route in the year 399. Paper reached Samarkand in 731, Damascus in 793, Egypt in the year of 900, Morocco 1100, Spain 1150, France 1167, Cologne 1320 and it arrived in England in 1494. Paper followed the same route as silk but at a much slower rate of speed.

People first looked after their food supply and their clothing supply before they put their minds to literature and art. And that is about the order of their importance and impact on civilization. First food, second clothing, and last and least art and literature. If you are to have an understanding of history this is the order in which to arrange your studies. Once we obtain a thoroughgoing knowledge of how man obtained his sustenance then we will be able to understand his art and literature. Teaching methods have skimmed over and in many instances ignored the fundamentals of man's existence and have emphasized art and literature as means of becoming educated. Many educators have recently complained that our primary schools are turning out a pack of illiterate juvenile delinquents that can't read or write. In fact, only a few years back a professor took the trouble to write a book called *Why Johnny Can't Read.* Although he did not underline the basic causes of our children's inability to read, his book became a best-seller.

Although the teaching process emphasizes reading, writing and arithmetic, there is no explanation of the why of their existence or why they became so widespread. The three "Rs" were and in some cases still are driven into children, and what is learned is painful indeed. Discipline has always been synonymous with education, that is why by the time most people reach mature years all spontaneity and abandonment have been driven out of them. Initiative is gone and they become efficient yes-men for the system that created them.

We owe to China the apricot, the peach and the oat, and to Southern India and China rice, to Southwestern Asia the sugar cane and the process for making sugar, and tea of course, to China alone. The idea which led the Arabs, the Sicilians and the Catalonians to the navigator's compass is of Chinese origin. China's contribution was the needle of magnetic iron which, thrust through a rice straw and floated in a bowl of water, furnished north and south directions. The Chinese used this method to re-survey the fields flooded each year by the Yellow River.

One of Persia's gifts to the world is domesticated alfalfa, or as the Persian word implies, "horse fodder." This fine hay is closely associated with the breeding of fine horses, for which Persia was famous. Mention of this plant occurs in Aristophanes' play "The Knights" written in the year 424 B.C., in which he refers to alfalfa as medic grass from Media. Alfalfa was known in Italy as early as the second century B.C., but it was also known in Assyria according to a translation of a Babylonian text as early as 700 B.C. King Korasan of the Assyrian dynasty was an up-to-date political economist with emphasis on the *political*. He knew how to raise money by taxation. He taxed the most useful and profitable things.

Persia had a great trade in fine horses. These horses were fine because they were fed on alfalfa. Hence Korasan taxed an acre of alfalfa seven times as much as an acre of barley or wheat. Persian men did not bring the high prices of Persian horses, therefore their food was taxed less than the food of horses. The same general principle applies to our modern tax on gasoline. The emperor Wu, was not indifferent to the beauty of Fergana and Persia. He sent ten expeditions to Persia to buy horses. One of his commissioners, General Cankeen, stole some alfalfa seeds and brought them back with him to China, shrewdly reasoning that a good horse needs good fodder.

We were not able to learn why the Romans associated wine with "truth" but we do know that the grapevine and the gracious art of wine-making are among the oldest of man's agricultural efforts. Only the cultivation of cereal grains are the more ancient. This speaks well for the social life of Antiquity. Wine and grapes were known to the Egyptians 4,000 years before Jerusalem Slim pulled his stunt of turning water into wine at the wedding in Cana. Brother Noah of Bible fame was a wine imbiber and drunk most of the time. Armenia has been suggested as the first home of the wine makers. The honor has also been claimed for the Hindus. Some historians are willing to concede the honors to the Jews as the originators of the art of wine-making. However, without regard for racial affinities, wine and grapes belong to western Asia Minor.

The wines and grapes of modern France and Germany were planted by the Greeks in Gaul before Caesar decided to make it a part of his empire. The Persians were the most famous wine drinkers of antiquity.

Even after the Koran forbade it they did very well, as the talkative and melodious old Omar Khayyam, with his loaf of bread, his tree, and his jug of wine, yields ample proof.

The Greek historians of the time of Alexander the Great were shocked at the Persian parties, but as history records, Alexander got the idea himself. If there was a wild party going on anywhere he wanted to be in on it. Alexander conquered Persia, but Persian wine conquered him. The Persians were as famous for their fine wines as for their horses, gold brocades, steel and ceramics, as this anecdote implies. The younger Cyrus, when he came upon an especially fine wine, used to send the half-emptied flagons to famous individuals with the following message: "For some time Cyrus has not found a pleasanter wine than this one, and he therefore sends some to you begging you to drink it today with those you love best."

PART IV

The preceding installment of this series ended with a quote from Cyrus the Younger, an ancient Persian ruler who sent half-empty flagons of wine to famous people telling them to share it with those they loved best. And, in case you didn't know it before, you now know who invented paper and how it was distributed throughout the world. This final installment discusses two kinds of wealth and their importance to civilization.

The so-called preference of Negroes for watermelon is probably founded upon a common origin; for watermelon, called "the melon of the west," originated in South Africa, spread up to Egypt and from Egypt to Anterior Asia, Persia, Turkestan and China. It is said of Catherine of Russia that she once sent Frederick the Great a crate of watermelons when he asked her for a province.

Twenty-four plants that at one time or another appear on our breakfast table traveled from China to Persia, and more than 60 from Persia to the western world. At the very dawn of sixteenth century there occurred one of the most fruitful exchanges of wealth within the history of the human race. For thousands of years the great food plants of Asia had been spreading over Africa and Europe. For thousands of years America, particularly the region bounded by Mexico on the north and Peru on the south had been domesticating a series of plants unknown to either Asia, Europe or Africa.

During the sixteenth century these annually recurring forms of wealth were exchanged, or rather multiplied by the most deliberate and purposeful diffusion the world was ever to know.

The two centuries that followed, the seventeenth and eighteenth centuries, are historically associated with many other comparatively trivial matters, such as Wars, Invasions, Conquests and Colonization. But the increase due to the worldwide exchange of domestic plants and animals in the sixteenth century has resulted in an absolute gain in world wealth—all areas of the world were better off, and to the extent that such constructive work in production was done, all peoples of the world are better off.

The historians lay much stress upon the flood of gold and silver which poured into Europe during the seventeenth and eighteenth centuries, upsetting all standards of values, causing an inflation due to the fourfold increase of silver and the somewhat less, but still vast increase of gold. These metals were used for the expenses of warfare, and supplied the munitions which eventually drove the Turks from Vienna and drenched the fields of Europe with blood. Silver and gold made Spain the richest and most modern of nations and then smothered her glory. The bullion looted from Mexico and Peru formed the liquid capital for the fruitful trade with the East that was inaugurated by Portuguese energy and Italian mathematical science.

In considering the wealth that men dig out of mines and the wealth yielded by husbandry and agriculture, we must bear in mind that agriculture is a recurring form of wealth ever renewing itself, but every ounce of silver or platinum, every pound of tin or copper, every gallon of oil, every ton of coal or iron men dig out of the bowels of the earth reduces by just so much the basic capital of civilization. Agriculture and herding under prudent and scientific management furnishes man with a more abundant life. The wealth of mines impoverishes one country and only temporarily enriches another, while the transfer of plants and animals makes each country or continent richer for the exchange. This method of reckoning refers to wealth, not to profit; to society, not to the individual.

Until the year 1500, no New World plants were known in the Old World, and no Old World plants were known in the New World. With minor qualifications this is true. There seems little reason to doubt that the Polynesian navigators and colonizers of the Pacific islands had touched at times upon the Pacific coast of Central and South America and borrowed the sweet potato and left behind the coconut. The coconut may of course have drifted here by accident. The other seeming exception, cotton, which was known before history in the Indus Valley and in Mexico and Peru and in the southwest United States, is only a confusion in terms. The cottons of the New and Old Worlds are distinct species. Fertile crosses cannot be made between them since the Asiatic type has 13 chromosomes in the seed cell and the American type 26 chromosomes. This fact is of great significance to the botanist, but it is not important to the economic historian.

In both sections of the world, and without the influence, direct or indirect, of diffusion, textile-minded peoples came upon these delicate seed hairs and invented identical mechanical methods to convert them into yarn and cloth.

The Old World sent a wealth of items to the New World, and a man named Elmer D. Merrill was so impressed by the number of plants and animals contributed by the Old to the New World that he compiled a list of them.

He said Eurasia, particularly Asia, as contrasted to America, yielded a very much larger number of basic food plants as well as more types of domesticated animals, including all breeds of cattle, horses, camels, buffalo, yaks, sheep, goats, swine, geese, hens and most kinds of ducks. All true cereals with the exception of Indian corn originated in the Old World, these including wheat, rye, barley, oats, millet, Italian millet, pear millet, sorghum, rice and other cereals of minor importance such as teff, ragi and coix. Among the Old World vegetables his list is a whopper, including the turnip, rutabaga, chard, mustard, radish, beet, parsnip, carrot, onion, leek, garlic, shallot, spinach, eggplant, lettuce, endive, celery, asparagus, artichoke, pea, soy bean, cow pea, chickpea, and pigeon pea, lentil, broad bean, hyacinth bean, taro, yam, sugar cane and squash.

Among the fruits Merrill lists apples, pears, plums, cherries, grapes, apricots, peaches, olives, figs, almonds, persimmons, quinces, pomegranates, melons and watermelons. We can add to his list fruits that originate in the tropics, such as bananas, coconuts, oranges, lemons, limes, dates, mangos and breadfruit. All these things—at least a greater part of them at one time or another, or in one or another form—contribute to our breakfast.

The point is, of course, that breakfast is one of the items of our culture, more significant than any lesson learned at school; the fact is that without it there would be no school and no lesson. Breakfast is commonplace and we take it for granted as an everyday occurrence in our lives, and think nothing of it. Yet as an item of culture it outweighs all the sermons that have ever been preached, or ever will be preached.

Long before dawn of every weekday morning hundreds of trucks and wagons loaded with farm produce converge on a central market to supply us with our breakfast day after day, and while little or no thought is given to the matter, this is the foundation upon which culture and civilization is built.

Go where you will and ask any man or woman what culture and civilization is, what are its products, and every one of them without exception will tell you it consists of religion, philosophy, education or some ideological fantasy. How we come to have such a perversion of value is for this writer one of the great mysteries about man's intellectual values. Stop and think of it for a minute and you will see that it is the commonplace, everyday, homely things that make for life and living.

The changes that man has made in seeking a living have been enormous, and the extent of them is a partial measure of man's mastery over nature. From the conch shell to the trans-world radiotelephone, from the sharpened stick to the tractor combine, from the water wheel to the hydroelectric generator, from the ox cart to the jet plane, can be traced step by step the progressive augmentation of man's power in the conquest of nature's multiple domains, narrowing the gap between his actual state and his ideal definition.

The great churchmen, the philosophers, politicians, statesmen—in short, the great talkers have gotten all the credit for having created civilization and culture. This is a misplacement of credit, an unsound judgement, a maladjustment of value. Man is a history-making animal, the creator, director and custodian of appropriate conditions in the social sphere; we cannot judge him without reference to the blood and fire, the poverty, pestilence, hatred and misery in which he has written his relations with his fellows. The Capitalist system is considered by many as man's supreme social achievement in history.

We take the view that, while the making of Capitalism is his latest achievement, it is by no means his final achievement in history-making. Man has made history, and taken by and large it has been bad history. It has been history-making by impulse, history-making without sufficient forethought, history-making without plan or purpose, and to make matters worse, man in his making of history has selected and worked with ideas, which by the way is the poorest material in the world to work with. If someone would, or could, work out a plan by which everybody could have a first-class breakfast every morning, we would have a real start in the making of a human world.

Industrial Worker, October, 19, November 2 & November 30, 1959

The Struggle Continues
(linocut by Carlos Cortez)

THE WORLD IS HIS ORANGE
Labor Hands Over the Fruit of His Toil and
Then Gets About One-Eighth of the Juice
(cartoon by Art Young)

NOTES ON THE AUTHORS

Songwriter, poet, humorist, pamphleteer, and author of the most popular and longest running column in the IWW press, **T-Bone Slim (Matt Valentine Huhta)** is widely regarded as the union's single greatest "man of letters." Of Finnish descent, he was born and raised in Ashtabula, Ohio, and took up hoboing in his early manhood, working as logger, camp cook, harvest hand, construction worker and, in his last decade, as barge captain on the Hudson River. He died in New York in 1942. The many songs he contributed to the Little Red Song Book have been recorded by Utah Phillips, Joe Glazer, Pete Seeger, Faith Petric and many others. Some of his tall tales, rants and maxims ("Half a loaf is better than no loafing at all"; "Only the poor break laws—the rich evade them") are collected in the book *Juice Is Stranger Than Friction: Selected Writings of T-Bone Slim*, edited and introduced by Franklin Rosemont (Charles H. Kerr, 1992).

Well-remembered in IWW history as artist and cartoonist, **Leland Stanford Chumley**—Fellow Workers called him Lee—also served as the union's leading organizer of restaurant and other food-industry workers in the late 1910s and early 20s. In 1928, during the union's decline following the disastrous split of 1924, the one-time stagecoach driver opened a small restaurant of his own in Greenwich Village, which was for years a meeting-place for Wobs, other radicals and well-known writers and artists. Chumley died in 1935, but his restaurant is still thriving today.

Although little is known about **Jim Seymour**, he was one of the IWW's best known hobo poets, and widely published in the union's press. His most popular poem, "The Dishwasher," appeared frequently in the *Industrial Worker*, reprinted by popular demand. In 1919-20 he lived in Los Angeles and contributed several poems and articles—among them, "R-R-R-Raw Food"—to *The New Justice*, a pro-IWW socialist magazine edited by Clarence Meily, author of the Marxist classic, *Puritanism* (Charles H. Kerr, 1911). Later in the decade Fellow Worker Seymour settled in Chicago, where he became one of the central figures at Bughouse

Square. Some of his poems were collected in George Milburn's *The Hobo's Hornbook* in 1930.

One of the IWW's top soapboxers from the late 1920s on, **Jack Sheridan** (1905-1967) was an important link between the revolutionary industrial union movement and the creative hobohemia that gave the Chicago Renaissance much of it vitality and renown. Well known as the "Poet Laureate of Chicago's Bums," Sheridan was a "regular" at Bughouse Square and—according to the *Sun-Times*—"for years the park's leading hobo poet." He was also a major figure at the Dil Pickle ("the indoor Bughouse Square"), and played a key role in the early history of Slim Brundage's College of Complexes. Fellow Worker Sheridan's good friends included such outstanding Wobs as Ralph Chaplin, Ben Fletcher, and Fred Thompson, as well as numerous poets, writers and artists, including Max Bodenheim, Ben Reitman, The Sirfessor (F. M. Wilkesbarr), Ric Riccardo and Frederick Pohl.

The "Food Question": As It Was, As It Is
(*One Big Union Monthly*, November 1919)
(cartoon by Joe Hill)

Preamble of the Industrial Workers of the World

The working class and the employing class have nothing in common. There can be no peace so long as hunger and want are found among millions of working people and the few, who make up the employing class, have all the good things of life.

Between these two classes a struggle must go on until the workers of the world organize as a class, take possession of the earth and the machinery of production, and abolish the wage system.

We find that the centering of the management of industries into fewer and fewer hands makes the trade unions unable to cope with the ever growing power of the employing class. The trade unions foster a state of affairs which allows one set of workers to be pitted against another set of workers in the same industry, thereby helping defeat one another in wage wars. Moreover, the trade unions aid the employing class to mislead the workers into the belief that the working class have interests in common with their employers.

These conditions can be changed and the interest of the working class upheld only by an organization formed in such a way that all its members in any one industry, or in all industries if necessary, cease work whenever a strike or lockout is on in any department thereof, thus making an injury to one an injury to all.

Instead of the conservative motto, "A fair day's wage for a fair day's work," we must inscribe on our banner the revolutionary watchword, "Abolition of the wage system."

It is the historic mission of the working class to do away with capitalism. The army of production must be organized, not only for the every-day struggle with capitalists, but also to carry on production when capitalism shall have been overthrown. By organizing industrially we are forming the structure of the new society within the shell of the old.